M000314907

Reflections

The Story of Dorothy Swanson, wife of an 82nd Airborne Paratrooper

Cynthia A. Sandor

Library of Congress Control Number: 2020910542

Published by:

Cynthia A. Sandor
427 Oakleaf Blvd.
Oldsmar, FL 34677
813-895-2516
www.cynthiaasandor.com

ISBN: 978-0-999-7550-2-0

Available in eBook ISBN: 978-0-999-7550-3-7

Edited by: Jeanne M. Onuska – European Military History Museum

Book Design: Sharon Brownlie – https://aspirebookcovers.com
First Printing in the United States of America – 2020
10 9 8 7 6 5 4 3 2 1

TABLE OF CONTENTS

With frankness tempered by sensitivity, Sandor renders the true story of a woman's untiring faithfulness in her intrinsic worthiness and her heroic strivings toward personal actualization. –Linda Lee Greene, author of *A Chance at the Moon*

Dorothy Swanson and I have quite a lot in common. Although I did not arrive in England until 1948, when I was ten, my experiences as a refugee were equally tumultuous. Like Dorothy, I ran the gamut of being 'filthy foreign goods in an orphanage, a textile weaver at fifteen to becoming an actress, a writer for the BBC, and an international author. As it was for Dorothy, every step forward was a milestone achievement. I recommend Dorothy's book to everyone who understands that a hard climb uphill is exhausting but the view from the top are usually worthwhile.

~ Elin Toona Gottschalk ~

English, Estonian and American author. "Into Exile: A Life Story of War and Peace"; nominated Best Memoir of 2013 by The Economist Magazine , Recommended Reading by The US Review of Books 2015, Erik Hoffer Grand Prize Finalist 2016 and many other awards.

I dedicate this book to Norman.
Thank you for your service.

Acknowledgement

It takes a creative and dedicated group of individuals to bring a book to life. I am grateful to Dorothy R. Swanson for entrusting me to write her memoir.

Special thank you goes out to my editor Jeanne M. Onuska – European Military History Museum and graphic designer, Sharon Brownlie from Aspire Book Covers for capturing the essence of the story.

Before WWII – 1936

ON AUGUST 2, 1936, with the help of a bottle of gin my mother drank to ease her labor pains, I was born on Cleveland Street. I am a trueborn "Bow-bell Cockney," a pejorative term applied to all city-dwellers located within the historical area of the church of St. Mary-le-Bow in London. The church was rebuilt after the Great Fire of 1666. Legend has it, if you were born within the sound of the church; you are a genuine "Cockney." The term 'cockney,' comes from the word 'cock-egg,' which means 'a malformed egg.' In the old days, country-folk used to call people from the city, 'cockney,' because they were ignorant of country life.

Rosie is my nickname. I rarely go by Dorothy. My full name is Dorothy Rose Marie Roberts. I am the first of three children born into my family. My brother, William Blair, was born in 1938, and my sister, Gloria Norma Jean, was born in 1941.

At the time I was born, my parents, Dorothy and Earnest, lived together. They were not married. They married in Marylebone, London in 1939 when I was three years old.

By day, my father was a fish-fryer, and by night, a singing comedy cartoonist. His full name is Earnest

"Ed" Roberts, and his stage name was Eddie Royal. His friends knew him as Ed.[1] My father performed at various men's clubs around the area, including the Garrick Theatre, which is located within the city of Westminster. To build up the spirits of the people after the Battle of Britain, the Garrick Theatre reopened its doors when the Blitz ended in May 1941.

The theatre got its name from David Garrick, who was a prominent actor during the 1740s. He is partly responsible for how the theatre operates today. He revolutionized acting by playing his characters more realistically, and his performance as Richard III, was allegedly the first attempt at realism. Built in 1889, the Garrick Theatre honors David Garrick's legacy.

When I was five years old, I would accompany my father on many occasions to watch his shows. I remember walking into the theatre. The floor in the entrance hall had mosaic tiles, and the walls were of highly polished walnut panels. Four marble pilasters projected from the walls and large mirrors in decorative reliefs hung between them. When I sat inside the theater, I was in awe by the sight of its architectural style with its gold leaf accent around the stage and its plush red velvet seats.

I was so excited when the announcer walked out onto the stage and said, "And now for our next performance! The amazing singing cartoonist, Eddie

---

[1] Earnest "Ed" Frank Roberts – born Feb. 27, 1913, Islington, London, England – Died: 1972– Milton Keene Keys, England

Royal!" Everyone applauded. I clapped enthusiastically and told the people sitting next to me, "That's my Dad. That's my Dad!" I laughed with the other patrons throughout his performance and gave him a great big hug after the show.

My mother's name was Dorothy and everyone called her "Dolly."[2] I named my Cockapoo after her. She was born in London on May 30, 1918. At first, she was a loving mother and always kept the family stable. She was a server at the Bow Bells pub and worked six days a week, up to ten hours a day. I did not see much of her.

[2] Dorothy Ada Cronin Roberts-Mother's maiden name: O'Sullivan

The Beginning of World War II

1939

I WAS THREE years old when WORLD WAR II began on September 7, 1939. One year later, the German Luftwaffe systematically bombed London for fifty-seven days and nights. Most notably, was the large daylight attack against London on September 15, 1940. This vicious attack on my country became known as "The Blitz." It was a horrible time. I was not in London because my parents sent me away.

On the morning of August 31, Prime Minister Winston Churchill gave the orders for all children, expectant mothers, and the infirmed, to evacuate the following day. Seared in my memory is the day I left my family. It was a frantic day. The epic logistical challenge required thousands of volunteers to assemble over 1.5 million people. The process alone in London involved teachers, local authority officials, railway staff, and 17,000 members of the Women's Voluntary Service. Together, they provided assistance, refreshments, and looked after apprehensive and tired evacuees at the railways stations.

I assembled with the other children and their parents at the school. A name card was pinned to the lapel of my coat. It contained my name, my school, and evacuation point. My suitcase contained one change of clothing, my nightclothes, a pair of socks, my toothbrush, a comb, towel, soap, a face cloth and a handkerchief. I wore my winter coat. I saw brothers and sisters clutching each other's hands. Children lined up in the school halls getting ready to leave. An adult told me that I would separate from my siblings. Etched in my memory are the words "I'll have that one." My mother clutched me tightly in her arms. She bent down, looked me straight in my eyes and said, "Not to worry my dear, you'll be home soon. You are going on a short field trip with your friends."

With my little suitcase in hand and holding a box containing a gas mask, I left my home in Islington. I remember singing. I think it was to keep up our spirits. I wondered where I was going on this great big adventure. My mother could not conceal her tears. Operation Pied Piper is the name of this great exodus. I was one of the millions of children who fled into the countryside to be safe from Hitler's Luftwaffe.

I boarded the railway car in Paddington. As the train rolled slowly away from the station, we sang "Wish Me Luck as You Wave Me Goodbye." I remember the lyrics to this day:

"Wish me luck as you wave me goodbye,
Cheerio, here I go, on my way.
Wish me luck as you wave me goodbye,
Not a tear, but a cheer, make it gay.

Garth Hill – 1945

I LIVED WITH my family in a small cottage in Garth Hills, Wales. I was eight years old when my mother began to beat me. I did not know what happened to her to turn her into such an abusive woman. Looking back at it, I think she may have had PTSD. She never told me what happened to her or my father during the war. My brother, William, and my sister, Gloria, were also abused, beaten with a coat hanger that was as strong as steel.[3] Even today, my brother bears the scars on his back.

It was right before the end of the war in 1945 that we left Garth Hill. My parents could no longer afford to take care of us. My brother, sister and I, moved in with my mother's sister, Aunt Rose, and her husband, Uncle Alf, in Braughing Friars. My parents were unemployed and had no money. My aunt and uncle were wealthy and had a small cottage they rented to my parents on the east side of Hertfordshire, in Puckeridge. I was eight years old. Billy was seven, and Gloria was four years old. My aunt and uncle were childless and at first, welcomed us into their home. My aunt always told me that if I were a good girl, Uncle Alf would leave

---

[3] William Blair Roberts, Gloria Norma Jean Roberts

everything to me in his Will.

Instead of living in a loving household, I went through some horrible experiences, things a child should never endure. My aunt physically abused me while my uncle sexually abused me. When I told my aunt what he did to me, she screamed, and told me I was a liar. When she mentioned this to my uncle, he viciously denied it. I wanted to leave their house and move back in with my parents rather than having his hands all over me. It was not until sometime later on that I found out that our living arrangements were pre-arranged. My brother, sister, and I worked at my aunt and uncle's restaurant called, The 46th Cafe. The money we earned paid for our parents' rent.

My Aunt Rose was a real die-hard Italian. I overheard a conversation she had with a neighbor. My aunt told her how proud she was for sending money and jewelry to that fascist dictator Mussolini. I wondered how I could get rid of them and then, I came up with a brilliant idea. I called the police and I told them that my aunt and uncle were using a flashlight to send Morse code messages to someone out in the woods. The police arrived and questioned my aunt and then myself. I do not know where my uncle was. After the police left, Aunt Rose tied me to a Damson tree, and whipped me with one of the branches. I stayed there for the rest of the day, tied to the tree just like a Billy goat. I was in so much pain, I cried, asking God, "Why is this happening to me?"

It did not help when I called the police a second time on Uncle Alf. This time I wanted to get rid of that damn tree. I told the police that my uncle buried my aunt under it. The police came and dug the soil up around the tree. I had lied and that did not help either.

Between 1939 and 1945, Britain was home to more than 400,000 prisoners of war from Italy, the Ukraine, and Germany. Housed in hundreds of camps around the country, some prisoners were in Braughing, right at the end of the lane where we lived.

I do not know how she did it, but Aunt Rose was able to get word to some of the Italian POW'S inside the camp. They slipped out of camp and ate at our house. I guess she made friends with one of the guards, because one day, I walked inside the house, and saw these men sitting at the kitchen table eating.

The prisoners wore old uniforms with black patches sewn on the legs and backs, which allegedly were targets should a prisoner try to flee. In many camps, ardently pro-fascist captives were required to wear black armbands denoting their propensity to continue to 'fight the war' from behind enemy lines.

For the most part, I heard the prisoners were content with their version of British life. They turned their camps into temporary homes and sometimes built a chapel or a 'memorial to life' in honor of their homelands. In the center of town, one group of Italians built a monument to Marconi.

The Geneva Convention ensured that prisoners of

war be treated fairly and received the same rations as ground troops. Britain treated the German POW's fairly so that the German authorities had no reason to mistreat British prisoners on German soil. Aunt Rose fed the prisoners until they could not eat anymore. At dusk, they would sneak back into their camps.

One time as I walked along the road, I saw camp guards proceed straight to our house! Aunt Rose must have known something was happening, because the men had left right before the guards stormed into the house!

"Where are they?" one of the guards yelled.

"I don't know what you are talking about," Aunt Rose said as she was washing the dishes. Afraid, I huddled in the next room and peaked around the door to see what was happening. Nobody noticed me.

"We know they were just here! Don't you realize that they are prisoners of war and are not allowed to be in your house?" the guard yelled as he looked around the room. Then, the guard's tone of voice changed. He seemed a bit more compassionate. "We don't mind if they visit you, but outside only, and, if you want to, you can throw food over the fence for them. But, they are not allowed to come inside your home!" the guard commanded.

Aunt Rose nodded in agreement and profusely apologized. As the guards left the house, she closed the door behind them, and breathed a sigh of relief. She turned and looked at me. I ran away as fast as I could.

I guess Aunt Rose said something to the prisoners, because the next time they came to the house, one gave me a hand-carved wooden doll. It was made out of scrap wood and material they found in camp. I was so happy. This was my very first toy.

Sometimes, the neighborhood kids and I gathered apples from the orchard, walked down the street, and tossed them over the fence. The prisoners thanked us in Italian, "Grazie! Grazie!" and smiled at us. We told them we would be back as soon as we could return.

England was still very much at war with Germany. German dive-bombers flying in Skukas, and the machine-gunning hedgehoppers, flying the FW-190's, strafed to strike any moving person.

One day while on the path between The 46th Café and the house, I heard the roar of airplane engines overhead. In a panic, I ran to get out of the way. I tripped and fell into a mud-puddle. The pilot must have had children, because, for some reason, he did not shoot at me. When I looked up, I saw him wave.

Another time, Uncle Sid, came to meet me at school. He was not my real uncle but rather a friend of the family. We left the building and we heard a plane heading our way. He screamed for me to jump. I froze in place. He jumped into the ditch and the pilot shot bullets at him. Unscathed he got up, brushed the dirt off his trousers, waved his fist high into the air, and yelled, "Those damn Nazis can go to hell! They're not going to get me!"

One evening we were sitting around the radio listening to Winston Churchill speak, "Never, never, in nothing great or small, large or petty, never give in, except to convictions of honor and good sense."

"If those damn Nazis get here, we'll put our heads in the oven and gas ourselves!" Uncle Alf proclaimed to Aunt Rose as she sat there nervously knitting.

I remember listening to Lord Haw-Haw on the radio. Lord Haw-Haw was a nickname applied to the U.S.-Born Briton, William Joyce, who disseminated Nazi propaganda to the UK from Germany by radio. The broadcasts opened with "Germany calling! Germany calling!" He spoke in a perfect upper-class English accent and told us where the Germans were going to bomb. Towards the end of the program, he laughed and said, "You might as well give up right now!"

Those Germans were smart and they used propaganda to try to make us surrender. "Germany Calling" reached audiences in the UK via medium radio waves over the Reichssender Hamburg radio station and by shortwave radio to the United States. Through such broadcasts, the Reich's Ministry of Propaganda, headed up by Joseph Goebbels, attempted to discourage and demoralize American, Australian, British, and Canadian troops, plus the British population, by suppressing the effectiveness of the Allied war efforts. They tried to maneuver the Allies toward peace terms that would leave the German regime intact and in power. Among the many techniques they used were tallies of Allied planes shot down and ships sunk. All during the war, reports of high Allied materiel losses and human casualties were discouraging. Uncle Alf and Aunt Rose knew they were propaganda and tried to explain it to us. The broadcasts were the only sources available from behind enemy lines concerning the fate of friends and relatives who had not returned from bombing campaigns over Germany. We frequently listened to Lord Haw-Haw's broadcasts despite the infuriating content, the frequent inaccuracies, and the exaggerations in the hope of picking up clues about the fates of our own and our Allied troops.

We also listened to a Japanese propaganda program given the name of "Tokyo Rose," by American troops stationed in the South Pacific during the war. Contrary to popular belief, there was not an English-speaking Japanese female at the microphone, but rather, a selection of them at different times. The propaganda broadcasted tried to demoralize the Allied forces abroad and their families at home by emphasizing the troops' wartime difficulties and losses. I remember Tokyo Rose said, "Give up the fight boys! Return home to your wives and mothers. You're not wanted here anymore." To ease the pain of war, a special song played at the end of the nightly broadcasts called, 'Goodnight Children Everywhere.'

"Sleepy little eyes in a sleepy little head,
Sleepy time is drawing near.
In a little while you'll be tucked up in your bed,
here's a song for baby dear."

The United States Army Air Forces (USAAF) set up an operational training base located forty-five miles south-west of us in Bovingdon, Hertfordshire. It operated from 1942 until the end of the war. It never developed into a fully-fledged heavy bomber airfield, as it did not have the required 2000-yard runway. Most of the combat bombers who arrived in Britain trained at the base for operations in the European Theater. For military operations, the Americans took over my aunt and uncle's property against their will. I do not remember which division or regiment it was. I remember the command bunker was located on High Street in Ware, in the next village from us, to coordinate local defenses, and respond to the air raids.

On some occasions, my mother came to visit us. When my aunt first told my mother about the soldiers on the property, she became frightened. My mother thought the reason why they were there was because the Germans would start bombing our little village. I could not understand why my mother was so upset because I thought they were there to protect us. I remember seeing Aunt Rose become upset with the soldiers. Why I do not know, but with a stern look on her face, she stood right up against the major and said,

ground, and began to cry.

I loved my two pigs, Margaret and John. Margaret was a British Lop pig. She had a long and fat frame and her ears hung over her face. John was a medium-size Welsh pig with a long and lean body. One day, Uncle Alf and a neighbor tried to put Margaret into the back of a truck. They lost their hold and she escaped! Billy, Gloria, and I were screaming "Run, Margaret, run!" We were so happy when she got away. Eventually, the men caught her and carted her off in the back of the truck. We never saw Margaret again. I was heartbroken.

Uncle Alf did not sell John because he was too skinny. John lived a comfortable life in the back yard and ate the plums and apples that fell from the trees. All day long, John would eat and sleep, and roll in the mud. My uncle tried desperately to thicken him up, but he always stayed thin. I did not eat pork for years afterward.

The following spring, my aunt and uncle planted a beautiful vegetable garden with a large sweet corn field. That was the first time I ate corn on the cob. It tasted delicious!

Finsbury Park – 1948

FOOD RATIONING EXTENDED nine years after the war, and in some aspects, became stricter. The European economy was slowly recuperating and a new era emerged. The rise of two superpowers became competitors on the world stage and the Cold War began. We had no comforts or luxuries, because resources were not available to expand food production, and no one was available to work on the farms. There were many strikes throughout London, and when someone died, the family kept their ration booklet to use for themselves instead.

The most controversial was when the so-called 'national loaf' of whole-meal bread replaced the ordinary white variety. It looked wretched, and it was gray, not like the real white bread. It was mushy and tasted horrible. Because of it, I had digestion problems. It would not be for another year until I would eat real white bread again.

By 1948, the war had been over for three years. Great Britain won two bronze medals in the 1948 Winter Olympics and three gold medals during the Summer Olympics. A new 'look' in women's fashions became available in the stores, and our own John Derry became the first British test pilot to break the sound barrier by flying in a de Havilland DH 108.

I was twelve when Uncle Alf and Aunt Rose sold

The 46th Café. They started a new restaurant on the corner of 72 Evershot and Thorpedale Roads in Finsbury Park, London. Once again, I was working for them, as a server. My job was to memorize and call in the orders. We always had a full house and I had to be on top of my game at all times. I could not slack off.

The restaurant was very popular and porters from the Finsbury Park train station would come over regularly to eat. I remember one morning, a porter ordered steak and eggs. I gave it to him and went on to the next customer. The porter ate the meal and he placed the plate onto another table. I forgot that I previously served him, and I made the mistake of giving him another meal. He ate that too!

"Pick-up!" yelled Uncle Alf through the window putting the plate on the shelf for me to grab.

I walked up to him and said, "I think you already gave that to me."

"Hey! Where's my steak and eggs?" yelled a customer from a few tables down.

"Are these steak and eggs?" I asked Uncle Alf.

"No! Its steak and kidney pudding" he retorted.

Realizing my mistake, I gave the second customer's steak and eggs to the porter! Uncle Al was upset with me because he had to make another steak and egg meal on the fly! Even though the customer was patient and understanding, I did not receive a tip from him. I was not so lucky, though, because the loss of the meal came out of my wage. I received five shillings a week, which is equivalent to $0.3 in today's currency.

At home, I placed my tips and wages into a candy box, and hid it underneath my bed. When I had enough money saved, I bought a new pair of shoes and a dress.

One day, I carried twenty pounds of horsemeat from the butcher on Marylebone Road, close to where Sherlock Holmes had his office on Baker Street, back to the restaurant. The butcher wrapped the meat tightly in thick, brown paper and tied a string around it. I grabbed the meat and raced back to the restaurant.

By the time I walked through the Ware Railway Station, blood seeped through the bag, and all over my dress. I handed the bloody package to Uncle Alf.

"You didn't let the porters see you did you?" He snorted.

"Of course they saw me! I told them the meat was for your dogs!" I sarcastically remarked back to him.

I watched Uncle Alf as he cut off the yellow fat from the horsemeat. To remove the gamey taste, the meat sat for days in a vinegar and white rum marinade, with oil, and finely chopped onions, salt and pepper, and a clove of garlic. Patrons thought they were eating real beefsteak! Uncle Alf always kept a strip steak on a plate in the icebox to show just in case anyone complained. My stomach turned when I saw Uncle Alf squeeze lemon juice on the hair growing from the horsemeat just before he cooked it. "Look at those idiots eating," he said with a smirk on his face. "They don't even know what they are eating!" he said while standing back with his arms proudly crossed over his chest. This shows you just what kind of a man he was.

Another two years went by and I was still working at the restaurant. At fourteen, I was an impressionable young girl. One day, a man walked in, and his appearance was deceiving. He wore a smart tweed suit with a white shirt, a black tie, and heavy black-rimmed glasses. His receding hairline made him look distinguished. I walked up to him, took his order, and we began to converse. He did not speak much louder than a whisper. I leaned over and strained to hear him speak.

"Have you ever read *Christ in Concrete*?" he asked.

"No," I replied.

"I have a copy of the book at my home. After lunch, would you like to come home with me, and we can read it together?" he asked.

"Ah..." I hesitated, and thought quickly, "I can't. I have to work."

I immediately ran to my great aunt Julie, Uncle Alf's mother, who worked at the restaurant. I told her about the strange conversation I had with this man.

"*Do not* go to that stranger's house," she sternly advised. "You don't know who he is or what he may do to you. Tell him no! If he says anything to you, you come to me, understand!" Aunt Julie ordered.

I was so happy that she talked me out of it because I was going to go to his house after work. I felt a sigh of relief when he paid for his meal and left.

The next day, that same man made the front page of the paper. His full name was John Reginald Halliday Christie, known to his family, and friends as Reg Christie. He was an English serial killer. I read that a man by the name of Evans, his wife, and baby daughter, lived with Christie at his house in Notting Hill. The day before, the police discovered the bodies of Evan's wife and his child. The police arrested Evans and sent him to prison. Christie was a major witness for the prosecution and the court found Evans guilty. Evans execution was immediate.

Three years later, the police discovered Christie was the true murderer. The London Police seriously mishandled the original inquiry as well as their investigation. Their incompetence during the search of the house on Rillington Place, allowed Christie to escape detection, and enabled him to murder four more women.

Christie hid the bodies in the wallpaper-covered alcove in the kitchen, outside in the garden, and his wife's body beneath the floorboards in the front room. When the police found the bodies, Christie confessed to killing Evan's wife, but not the others. Christie hanged for his crime.

The police exhumed Evan's body and immediately returned it to his parents for a proper burial. I do not believe the police compensated the family for what they had done. I think all his parents received was an apology.

My days working at the restaurant ended and I returned home to live with my parents. I started working at the optical factor, C.W. Dixey & Son. I was in charge of polishing Winston Churchill's infamous Cartwell tortoise-shell, double-dot motif glasses. I felt honored to hold such a prestigious position at such a young age.

The next position I held was at W.S. Fordham's Haberdashery, in Puckeridge, on the east side of Hertfordshire. It was located on High Street in the London House, and carried all sorts of items like furniture, and drapery. Fordham's sold items used in sewing and since I was a retail clerk, I learned everything about notions.

Behind this quiet village in Puckeridge is a colorful history, which dates as far back as three-hundred BC when Celts from northern Europe first settled in the area. They built the trade roads from Puckeridge to St. Albans and from Colchester to Baldock. The Romans, and then the Saxons, later occupied the town. The Saxons gave this village the name 'Devil's Hill.'

Puckeridge is nestled in the valley of the Rib and protected from the extremes of weather. Nearly everyone has well water and the ground was very fertile too. For the last 1000 years, Puckeridge had made its money from wheat and barley.

The main street called the High Road is the trunk road for the grain wagons trundling to London. There are not many central landmarks here either. The village

was wearing overalls while the other girls were wearing dresses. I felt so embarrassed. I was in school for a year before I had to leave. My aunt and uncle could no longer afford to pay for my tuition. I wanted so much to return to school and receive an education. I found out that I could receive a scholarship to the pre-nursing school in Puckeridge, and I applied. I received a letter from the educational board saying that they approved my application. I was elated and shared the wonderful news with my parents. They told me I could not go to school because I had to work at the Mapleleaf Café to pay for their rent.

I hated working at that restaurant. I ended up working in the kitchen all day long peeling potatoes. I peeled so many potatoes that my skin was practically falling off my fingers! I was so happy the day I left and returned to school.

Meeting Norman – 1951

I WAS SO happy to return to Chestnut and complete my pre-nursing education. It was during this time that I first met my husband-to-be, Norman.[5] I was sitting on the bus, riding home, when he came up from behind, and sat down right next to me. He must have been sitting in the back because I did not notice him. We started talking, and from then on, he was on the bus everyday waiting for me. I remember my father's words clearly to this day.

"Rosie, don't ever get off the bus at Collier's End. That's where the American base is," he sternly said.[6] "You do remember what happened to your friend, Edna, don't you?" he asked.

"Yes, I remember," I bashfully responded.

Edna Stark was my best friend. We did everything together. I stopped socializing with her when I found out she became pregnant by a black aviator from the military base.

"Birds of a feather flock together," my father sarcastically remarked.

It was not until after she married, and had her child, that I was able to see her again. Nevertheless,

---

[5] Norman Raymond William Swanson
[6] Collier's End is a hamlet located in the area of Standon Parish, in Puckeridge. More historical information about Collier's End is located in the back of this book. There was a former army camp on Dowsett's Lane.

things changed, and our friendship fell apart. I never did see her again.

One day, I thought it was strange that Norman was not on the bus. As the bus stopped at Collier's End, a Hawaiian looking paratrooper boarded the bus and asked, "Is there a Dorothy Roberts here?"

I was so shy at the time that I did not raise my hand. I put my head down, looked out of the corner of my eyes, and saw the other people looking around.

"If there is a Dorothy Roberts here, please raise your hand! We have to be on our way!" the driver articulated in his heavy British accent.

Bashfully, I raised my hand.

The man walked over to my seat and said, "Your parents asked me to come and take you to the club."

I remember what my father said about not getting off at Collier's End.

"I don't know," I replied, questioning myself. "How did he know my name?" I trusted my intuition and left with this strange man.

He escorted me into the NCO club, and to my mother's table. My father was on stage performing. Out of the corner of my eye, I saw Norman. He was beyond intoxication. He stumbled over the chairs and into his friend's arms. He looked up from his drunken stupor, and started running towards me shouting, "Hey! That's my wife!"

I felt so embarrassed and made a mad dash for the door. Norman ran after me. My mother sat there with her whiskey in hand, watching the event unfold. She probably thought this scene was a slight diversion from watching her husband perform on stage. Norman's friends grabbed him.

"Swanny!" he hollered. "That's not your wife!"

Turning to me, another young paratrooper said, "Don't worry ma'am. We are going to take him over to the barracks right now."

Norman's head hung low and his arms hung over his buddy's shoulders. Grumbling, they carried him out of the club.

I sat down next to my mother and waited for my father to finish his performance.

"What the hell was that all about?" my mother asked.

"I don't know. He thinks I'm his wife," I answered.

After the show, my parents enjoyed a drink, and together we walked jovially home.

When I came home from school the next day, I opened the front door, and Gloria was waiting for me.

"A man is waiting for you in the living room," she whispered.

As I had never dated before, I was in shock to hear this announcement. I walked inside and found Norman sitting in the living room wearing his full military regalia. When he stood up, I noticed a shoebox in his hands.

"I heard I made a complete ass out of myself, so, I owe you an apology," he said, expressing himself in a most sincere display of affection I have ever witnessed by a man. My heart leaped in my chest.

"Here...," he bashfully spoke as he extended his arms out to me. "This is for you. Peace for a peach."

I slowly reached my hands out and accepted the box. I looked down and removed the top. I pushed the shavings off to the side, and to my delight, gazed upon this magnificent velvety, soft, fleshy red, yellow-orange oval shaped fruit. My mouth began to water! I was in shock to find this beautiful peach! Fresh fruit was difficult to come by.

"Your dad said I can take you to the movies tonight. Would you like to go?" he asked.

I did not understand what he said, "What's a movie?" I asked.

He laughed. "A movie?" he responded. "Oh, I forgot. You call them pictures over here. It's the same thing," he explained.

"Oh, I don't think I can go. My father told me that I shouldn't," I answered.

"But you can! I asked your father and he said it would be all right with him if you came out with me to the movies tonight. He said it would be good for you to get out of the house," he excitedly explained.

I set the box in my room, and off I went with Norman to the pictures.

He was a perfect gentleman. Looking dapper in what I called his 'Double-A' military uniform, we walked from the house to the theatre in Ware. I listened intently to him talk about his time in the 82nd Airborne Division, 327th Glider Infantry Regiment, to playing a pivotal role in Operation Market Garden, the airborne invasion of Holland.

"What a brave soldier he is," I thought to myself. The entire time, he chatted, and regaled me with his war stories. He landed on Utah Beach the day after D-Day, entered the front line, and crossed over the Douve River near Carentan, France. He told me how the First and Second Battalions guarded Utah beachhead's left flank northeast of Carentan. His Company, Company C was hit hard by enemy fire mortars while crossing the Douve. I was impressed when he talked about how his unit held off the Germans assuming the defensive sector south of Bastogne, to taking 750 German prisoners, knocking out 144 Panzers, and over 100 other enemy vehicles. The 'Bastogne Bulldogs,' motto became infamous with his unit.

I felt comfortable walking with him, but, when we arrived at the theatre, I felt awkward sitting next to him. I did not know what to say or how to behave. This was the first time I was out on a date and I did not want to upset the moment by telling Norman that I did not like horror movies.

We watched the "House of Wax" starring Vincent Price. During the scary parts, Norman tried putting his arm around me. I responded by moving away from him. After a few attempts, he asked me if I wanted to go home, and gratefully, we left.

"Can I come and see you tomorrow Rosie?" he asked, standing on the front porch.

"I don't know...I'll have to think about it. Let me go inside and ask my parents," I said.

My father was sitting in the living room reading the paper and listening to the radio.

"Norman wants to take me out tomorrow night. Is that alright with you?" I asked.

"Do you like him?" my father asked.

"He seems like a nice guy," I shyly replied.

"Did he lay a hand on you?" he asked, folding his paper off to the side looking at me straight in my eyes.

"No, not really. He was a perfect gentleman," I said with a lump in my throat. Anticipating my father's reaction, I waited and held my breath for a response.

"Ok. You may see him tomorrow," he said flipping his newspaper back into the reading position.

I walked outside and told Norman that it was all right for him to come over and pick me up tomorrow.

"Hot dog!" he exclaimed, pecking me on the cheek. "I'll be over tomorrow around six," he said as he bounced down the walkway with a skip in his step.

Later on, I found out that Norman supplied my parents with whiskey and cigarettes. My parents sold me out!

Bletchley – 1951

THIS WAS THE first time in my entire life that I truly felt happy. Every day after school, Norman met me on the bus and walked me home. We talked about all sorts of things. I particularly enjoyed talking about the books he had read. He opened my mind to new thoughts and new worlds. I thought it was unusual for him to be on the bus when I was coming home. He told me that he had 'plenty of time on his hands' because he ran the NCO club on Dowsett's Lane in Collier's End, and he could leave anytime he wanted.

Norman became a regular visitor at my parents' house and they enjoyed his company. My parents permitted me to see him even though I was 15 years old. I loved our long walks in the city of Ware. He showed me his command bunker, introduced me to his commanding officer, and showed me the grottos. We dated for six months, until his reassignment to Headquarters Company, 928th Engineer Aviation Group USAFE, in Vienna, Austria. Norman switched over to the 101st Airborne Division. His commander wanted him to attend language school. Norman spoke five languages fluently, and he was going to learn how to speak Korean. Before he left, Norman gave me his airborne wings. He told me to send them back to the base if I did not want to see him anymore. I never sent them back.

Over time, I forgot about Norman. Six months later, he appeared at the front door.

"I guess you want to see me again!" he gleefully smiled.

I did not have the heart to tell him that I lost his wings.

Norman was constantly at the house and stayed until the last bus left. Sometimes, he missed the bus, and had to walk two and a half miles back to base. Norman and I talked for hours. He told me about his life growing up in Chicago, watching television, and dancing in the nightclubs. He told me about his parents, Gunard and Frieda. In 1904, Gunard arrived in the United States via Ellis Island, and legally changed his name from Gerrad Svensson, to Gunard Swanson.[7] Svensson means the 'Son of Sven.' The name itself is Old Norse for 'Young man,' or 'Young warrior.' Swanson means swan, and originated as a nickname for a 'pure or graceful person,' qualities attributed to the swan. Employment came easier with his new name, and he felt as if he was a true American. Originally, my father-in-law was a tailor by trade. When he came to the States, he found work at the US Post Office in Chicago until he retired. My mother-in-law, Frieda, was a stay-at-home wife. Frieda was born in Chicago, and

---

[7] Gunard Swanson – 1850 – 1996, Born: Sweden, Buried: Concordia Cemetery, Forest Park, Cook, IL

her parents were of German ancestry.[8] Frieda's parents, Herman and Johanna, arrived in America in 1873 and 1884, respectively. Frieda had three brothers, William, Edward, and Arthur.

Norman and I dated for three years before he proposed to me. I was still living at my parent's house on 10 Hollinwell Close, Bletchley, in Milton Keynes.

"Norman's waiting for you in the sitting room," my sister Gloria, whispered, covering her mouth with her hands, giggling.

I walked into the living room. Norman sat presentably dressed wearing his blue shirt, dark blue trousers, and black ankle boots.

He stood up, walked over to me, and took both my hands.

"I have something for you, Rosie," he said, getting down on one knee. He opened the box. "Would you marry me?"

"No! I don't love you," I replied.

"In time our love will grow. You do not have to love me now, but you will love me later. I promise, I will take good care of you," he beseeched remaining on his knee.

"Well, if it's okay with my father, I'll marry you. Come back tomorrow and I'll give you my answer," I casually replied.

Norman slipped the ring on my finger. His dark

---

[8] Frieda Wians, 1896 – 1990, Buried: Concordia Cemetery, Forest Park, Cook, Illinois, United States

brown eyes gazed deeply into mine. I blushed and turned away.

"Picture time!" my sister excitedly said.

Norman sat down on the chair and I sat gracefully by his feet.

"Click!" the sound of the camera made as my sister took our photo, forever etched in time. I escorted Norman to the front door.

"Think about it," he said. He kissed me on the cheek and left.

I closed the door and turned around wondering how my life would be if I did marry him. A million questions raced through my mind. What will my parents say? Will I have to move to America? Can we stay here in England instead? Does he want children? How are we going to take care of the children? Slowly, I walked into the kitchen contemplating my future.

My parents were sitting at the table. My mother was knitting and my father was trying to read the newspaper. He was drunk. I saw the bottle of whiskey on the table. He reeked of alcohol.

"Norman just proposed to me. What do you think I should do?" I said, showing the beautiful diamond engagement ring to my mother. She was elated!

"You don't have to marry him, but don't give him back the ring either, if you decide you don't want to," my father sarcastically remarked.

No sooner did I look at my mother for approval when I felt my father's fist punch me hard in the face. I fell backward and hit my head on the cupboard. My lip split open and I blacked out. I do not remember anything until the following evening when Norman came to the house. I opened the door.

"What's wrong with your face?" he asked.

I told him what had happened the night before.

"You're not staying here a minute longer," he angrily snorted.

"Where can I go?" I cried.

"I have a place for us to go! Pack your bag! We're leaving this very instant!" he ordered.

I raced upstairs and packed what I could. I overheard Norman in the living room screaming, at my father. Shaking, I came down the stairs with my little suitcase and peered around the corner. Norman grabbed my arm and we hurriedly left my parents' house, leaving them to fight among themselves. We arrived at a little converted laundry mat in town that had bed-siting accommodations and kitchenettes for the G.I.'s. Five families lived in this building.

I did not like being home all alone while Norman was at the club working. Otherwise, everything was fine for the first couple of months. He was a perfect gentleman and took care of me. I made sure the flat was tidy. A warm dinner awaited him when he returned home for the evening.

One night, it was getting late, and his dinner was getting cold. I had no way to contact him on base. When he walked through the front door, I saw that he was inebriated. He coerced me into having sex with him. I had never slept with a man before. The first time was not a pleasant experience. Afterward, Norman wanted to have sex all the time. I said "no" until I broke down and gave in. I figured if we were going to be married, there would be no harm in having sex beforehand. That is not what happened next.

"Let's get married right now!" Norman said.

"Don't I have to get permission from your commanding officer?" I asked.

"Ah... yes, you do. Let's go right now," he said excitedly.

We arrived at the base in Bletchley Park and I received the commanding officer's permission. By train, we rode to the American Embassy in London, for our physical examination, and blood work. I told the nurse that I was in a sanitarium for tuberculosis. If the test returned with positive results, I could not marry Norman. Thank God, my TB tests were negative!

Runaway Marriage – 1955

TO SOME, LOVE in the 20th Century was to elope with your sweetheart in a runaway marriage. Norman and I held our secret wedding in the border town of Gretna Green, Scotland, in a decidedly un-romantic venue, in the sweaty, stifling shop of the local blacksmith. Our love forever professed no doubt from the more or less poetic idea of indissoluble bonds, forged in iron, over the anvil.

Under English law, non-royal English citizens under the age of twenty-one could not get married without a signed permission note from their parents. The couple had to publicly announce their engagement in their town so that others could object if need be.

On the other hand, Scotland had very different marriage laws. Couples over the age of sixteen could get married by a 'declaration,' meaning the couple only had to announce their vows in front of witnesses. Parental permission was not required.

We professed our ever-endearing love to one another reciting our wedding vows as best as we could. The priest, who was the blacksmith himself, had no formal qualifications to lead the marriage ceremony. He concluded the service by pounding the anvil with a heavy iron hammer, thereby, symbolically joining us together forever, the way a blacksmith joins metal together. I was eighteen and Norman was thirty-three years old.

"Right-O! Carry on!" the blacksmith announced. We kissed and lo-and-behold, we were married!

We returned to England and announced to my parents that we were married. My mother was delighted and embraced me with open arms. My father wanted a white wedding with all the trimmings. However, my parents could not afford to pay for my wedding. Norman appeased my parents and paid for everything from the wedding gown, to the flowers, and to the village hall where we held a large reception. The entire village turned out for our wedding.

On January 22, 1955, Norman and I were married a second time at St. Mary's Church in Collier's End, because my parents wanted to see me formally marry. Built in 1911 by Mr. Charles Pritlove, of Wadesmill, the church has a simple brick exterior. It accommodates up to 150 people. It consisted of a chancel, vestry, nave, west porch, organ chamber, an embattled tower, and a tapering upward spire. The vane of the spire is quite original, and holds the letter "M" pierced by a sword, thus being an emblem of one of the sorrows of the Blessed Virgin.

A marked feature of the church is the beautifully carved rood screen, and communion rails, works of H. Gilbert, of Ware. The local carpenter, Mr. Wickham, carved the oak panels on the altar. Seven large candlesticks, symbolic of the seven churches in the district, surround the east stained glass window.

"You may now kiss the bride," the pastor said. How befitting for my parents, because now, we are 'officially' married in their eyes.

Symbolizing the building of our new life together, we passed underneath an honorary arch of shovels, held up by Norman's paratrooper friends, formerly dressed in their uniforms. The entire village attended our reception held at the local hall. Norman hired the army band to play the music. We danced until midnight.

Norman and I married a third time at the Registry's Office in Cambridge because we failed to give the required 28-day notice to the Registry Office prior to being married at St. Mary's Church in Collier's End.

In July 1955, our first daughter, Teri was born in Cambridge. My parents were ecstatic. My parents became emotionally supportive and encouraged my new role in life as a mother. I was 18 years old.

Ten months later, Norman and I left for America.

Arriving in America – 1956

TRAVELING FIVE DAYS over the Atlantic on the USS General H.F. Hodges (AP-144), a Squier-class transport ship for the U.S. Navy during WWII, we arrived in the Brooklyn Navy Yard in May 1956.

It was raining heavily when we disembarked. I tried to keep little Teri's head dry the best I could. We took a cab to St. George's hotel in Brooklyn, N.Y., where we stayed for the next few days.

I did not think I had married the same man because when Norman returned from what he claimed to be a quick errand, he burst into the room wearing a loud, yellow and green Hawaiian shirt with a straw hat, smoking a cigar hollering, "We're in the land of sunshine!" I did not see any land of sunshine. For two days, all I saw was pouring rain.

The next day the sun shone and I could see the New York City skyline from our apartment window. Norman was in a particularly good mood and proclaimed, "I'm going to buy us a brand new car today!"

"You never owned a car in England. You told me you do not know how to drive. How are you going to buy a car? " I questioned.

"We are in America now! I'll have the salesman bring us back to the hotel," he answered.

Off to the dealership we went with Teri in tow. Norman fell in love with the first car he saw - a beautiful two-tone blue, 4-door Mercury sedan with a 312 horsepower V-8 engine, with an automatic transmission, a deep-dish steering wheel, and cloth seats. Norman purchased black and white seat covers to protect the material. He meticulously took good care of his cars.

Norman paid cash and as he had promised, the salesperson drove us back to the hotel. In return, Norman gave him money for the taxi fare back to the dealership.

The next day, Norman placed an advertisement on the bulletin board at the shipyard saying, "Anyone desiring transportation to Chicago, Illinois to please contact Sgt. Swanson."

Two single couples answered the notice. They took turns driving, and drove us to 3001 South Keeler Avenue in Chicago, where Norman's parents lived. We said our good-byes and off they went in a taxicab to wherever they were going.

Norman only spoke German with his parents. My father-in-law, Gunard, was a sweetheart. He was wonderful, but my mother-in-law, Frieda, took an immediate dislike to me. She turned to Norman, and said something that sounded like, "you should have married a German girl, not an English swine!" I understood a few words and realized what she had said.

"Don't take any notice of Frieda," Gunard said in his heavy Swedish accent as he was helping remove the suitcase from the car. "Frieda loved Norman's first wife.

She was German."

"First wife?" I questioned to myself. Norman never told me about a previous marriage. I wonder what else he had not told me.

Then, Frieda said something to Norman that made him angry. "Get your things, we're leaving!" he yelled. Gunard drove us to the hotel and returned home in a taxi.

The next day, Norman's brother, Clifford, arrived and taught him how to drive. The boys were gone most of the day while I stayed in the hotel room taking care of Teri. We did not go out to the park or explore the city. Instead, we stayed inside and watched television. I was fascinated with the variety of live programs the three stations offered, including Milton Berle, Sid Cesar, and the Ed Sullivan Show. Television introduced me to quiz shows, loveable characters, and game shows. Within a few short days, Norman had his driver's license, and we left to find a place for ourselves.

Chicago to Virginia – 1956

IN JUNE 1956, Norman received orders to Ft. Belvoir, in Alexandria, Virginia. His reassignment took him to serve in the 9829th Tech Service Unit, Corps of Engineer School, and gave him strict top-secret clearance. He could not tell me what he was working on. For any reason I needed him, I had to call a certain number, and tell whoever was on the line, that I needed him home.

The government realized I was not an American citizen. This did not make sense to me, though Britain and America were allies. Besides, I thought they performed a complete FBI background investigation on me before I became Norman's wife.

Norman transferred to another unit and he still had to perform his monthly parachute jumps to receive his jump pay.

With Norman gone during the week, I began to get restless. I wanted to find work. I found a baby-sitter for Teri and I started working in Alexandria, at a state mental hospital for the criminally insane.

All the rooms had locks on the doors. A nurse warned me never to go into a locked room without another employee present. Behind the metal door, a frail-looking woman, who I thought could not hurt a flea, peered through the window. She asked for a glass of water. I did not think any harm would come. "I'll bring you some water," I compassionately replied. Instead of heeding the nurse's warning, I unlocked the door, went inside the room, and handed her the glass. Unbeknownst to me, she had a bedpan full of urine. She hit me hard on my head and practically knocked me unconscious. Before she could escape, another attendant ran down the hall and saw what had happened. When I looked up, I noticed the patient pulled the radiator out from the wall. That is how strong she was. I never opened another door again without having a second person with me!

A woman who had burnt her children alive resided in the same ward. The courts pronounced her criminally insane. She did not like me even though I did everything in my power to make her as comfortable as possible.

A male patient took a liking to me. He kept stroking my arm and telling me how beautiful I was. Later on, I found out that this resident was dressed as a man, and under his nightgown, he was a woman! The attendant said, "Don't listen to her! Let's go!" I never did find out why she was locked up.

I worked at the hospital for six months before management noticed I was not a legal citizen of the United States. The Director of Administrations called me into his office and said, "We hate to lose you, Dorothy, but you can't work here until you become a legal citizen. When you make your citizenship, we'll hire you back."

I heard the Crownsville Hospital Center in Crownsville, Maryland, had openings. I desperately wanted to work. When I arrived, Mrs. Blaisdell, the Director of Nursing, interviewed me. She told me there were no job openings. I told her I would clean, and do anything they needed, that I need to work.

"Well, we have one opening, but I don't know if you want to work there," Mrs. Blaisdell said.

"I'll work anywhere!" I replied.

"Well, it's in the colored ward," she said. "You'll be the only white person in the ward."

I am not a prejudiced person and I accepted the $5.00 per hour position. It took some time to adapt to working in Ward North 1. Not only was I spat on by the patients, they called me rude names. Remember, at this time the Civil Rights Movement was occurring.

It took a little time but the residents became used to my presence. The black staff began to treat me well, because they saw I was there to work. I had nothing bad to say against them.

A black, pregnant woman came into the hospital. Since there were no rooms available, two nurses took her straight into the delivery room. That poor woman was alone in the room, screaming every time she had contractions. It was about two or three hours later that the baby started to crown. Finally, a nurse came into the delivery room.

"Here, take this!" the nurse shouted, practically throwing the baby at me. She would not cross the red line on the floor. The baby was bloody and wrapped up in a green towel. It was the cutest baby I had seen.

"Here, clean this up!" the nurse ordered.

I removed the mucus from the baby's mouth and nose. When I looked back at the nurse, I will never forget the venomous look on her face. That was my initial introduction to hate and racism.

I never had an easy time walking from North 1 to the lab in the white section of the hospital. Every time I walked through the white section, the nurses bullied me, and called me horrible names. As I walked down the hall, they shoved and pushed me. They even called me a 'Nigger Lover.'

"That's the bitch working on North 1," one of the white nurses commented to another, as I walked past her.

North 1 was the black section of the hospital and had room for 30 patients and we had 51 patients! People were in the hallways and there were two to three residents to a room. Overcrowding was a problem, and many disputes erupted, because these patients wanted to be the first in line for their pediatric, ob-gyn, surgical, or medical care.

At this time, I was working as a nurse's assistant. I was learning much from them. They noticed I treated them fairly, without prejudice, and I was there when they needed assistance. At this time, the nurses were Licensed Practical Nurses, who received their certificate through a correspondence course offered in the newspaper. One nurse, who befriended me, suggested I take the course because I can earn a better wage. However, having a baby at home, I could not afford to go to school.

Another time, a young black man came staggering through the back door. Someone yelled, "Come and get him!" A bullet pierced through his abdomen and blood was discharging out onto the floor. Two nurses ran over to him, brought the patient into a room, and immediately applied bandages. I never saw a doctor on staff.

Another black woman came into the center and gave birth to a six-month-old premature baby. The poor thing fitted into a kidney basin. The LPN came into the room and said, "She doesn't need this bastard. She's got seven kids at home." The nurse took the basin, and with the baby inside, threw it down the incinerator. Never in my life had I witnessed another person so willingly murder an innocent baby. I was in shock!

I reported the incident to Mrs. Blaisdell.

"What do you want me to do about it?" she coldly remarked.

Unfortunately, I could do nothing either because we were living during the time of racial segregation. I never said another word about the incident until now. Occasionally, I think about the baby and wonder, what her life would have been like today.

Early one morning on his way to work, Norman came to pick me up. He walked into the building and overheard the LPN's shouting out at me.

"Why are they shouting at you?" he asked.

"Because I am working in North 1, the colored ward," I replied.

"You're not working here anymore! We don't need the money that bad," he angrily remarked. Right away, he pushed me into the car, and we drove home. I never returned to the hospital and I never gave them notice. At this time, I thought Norman could be prejudiced. I remembered back upon my friendship with Edna. I offered to babysit for her six-month-old black child. Norman came home and saw the baby in my arms.

"What the hell is that?" he questioned sternly.

"I'm babysitting for Edna until she gets home," I innocently replied.

"Get that bastard out of this house immediately!" Norman ordered. It did not hit me at that time until I thought about it again. I finally realized that Norman was prejudiced.

I fired the babysitter, stayed home to take care of Teri, cooked, and made sure our place was tidy. It was not long before our second child, Wayne, was born. It was a cold day in January 1957. Norman was so proud of his first-born son. Come the following January, our third child, Barry was born.

Tacoma, WA - 1958

IN SEPTEMBER 1958, Norman received orders for Camp Page, Korea, where he served in the Regular Army, 226th Signal Company, 4th Missile Command. I was five months pregnant with our fourth child, and lived alone in Tacoma, Washington, with our children, Teri, Wayne, and Barry.

I felt ecstatic to find a letter from Norman waiting for me in the mailbox.

"Hello My Love,

I have some free time and I thought I would send you a quick letter. I miss you so much! How are the kids? How are you feeling?

We took the Troop Ship General Edwin D. Patrick from Oakland to Korea. It was a long voyage. I was rather hungry when we received orders to board the ship. I did however, find a nice little 'pod' to settle into and I even met some new buddies.

When they called 'mess' over the horn, I raced to the dining room. Well, let me tell you that was a big mistake, because the Sergeant selected the first 40 of us for KP duty, and we had to eat last. The Sergeant gave us the option of working mess duty for the remainder of the voyage, or stand watch — two hours on with four hours off, for twenty-four hours a day, or we can do clean up detail like mopping the floors or cleaning the heads every day! There were 80 of us to serve 1000 troops. We worked three meals on and were off for three meals. I decided that mess duty seemed like a good way to have something to do and still have time off to enjoy the view of the Pacific Ocean.

We had been on the water for days and there was absolutely nothing to do! The weather topside was dreary because it rained most of the time. I checked out the ship's library and it was very limited in its reading material. You know how I love to read. I had to stay out of the way of the other detailers, and I could not remain in my bunk to read either. Most of us were bored. We also had civilian passengers on board so we were restricted in our movements.

Working in the mess hall kept me busy. There were not enough trays, utensils, and space to feed the 1000 men on board all at the same time. The meals usually took four hours to serve from beginning to end because we had to inspect every single fork, knife, spoon, the glasses, bowls, and trays for particles. It seemed the Army did not want to get their soldiers sick in the middle of the ocean.

There was no alcohol available on the ship either. Movies were old and they only played at night. Do you know what you see in the middle of the Pacific? Water, water, and more water! The ocean seems like it goes on forever!

Excitement was abound when we spotted another ship or an island. Occasionally, one of those little storms came up and the ship would rock forward and backward, or from side to side. I saw some green soldiers.

We stopped overnight and disembarked at Pearl Harbor. I felt sad seeing the Arizona underwater.

We were back on the ship the next day. The mundane routine was broken when one of the men came down with spinal meningitis. Because of the seriousness of his illness, we were required to place curtains between the bunks. Our bunks are like little white banana pods, with six bunks on a pod, three high and three side-by-side. One guy's foot hung beside my head and another had his butt a few inches away from my nose. Fun, fun, fun! Sometimes, it stunk terribly at night when you got a good whiff of someone else's wind!

There was a diversion when the captain decided that the sick soldier be removed from the ship. A lot of us watched from topside as the stretcher came down from the helicopter to pick him up.

After an overnight stop in Japan to refuel, we finally arrived in Pusan, South Korea. I gathered my belongings, disembarked, and boarded the train for Seoul.

This train was built for shorter people, because there was very little knee room. It moved lazily between villages on our way to Seoul. I saw people living in grass-thatch huts along the side of the tracks. When the train stopped, the locals would run-up to the windows offering us food and trinkets. The Sargent warned us to decline anything offered to us from the locals. The kids seemed very friendly though, waving and saying "Hi, GI!" or "Hi Joe!"

The worst part of the trip was the wretched odor that emanated from every part of the train. We all wondered what had died.

Twelve hours later, we finally arrived in Seoul. I was parched and famished. It was late and the only building opened was the Enlisted Men's Club. I had a couple of drinks with my friends, and we slept well until 5:30 the next morning when the door busted open, and we were ordered to get up, get our shots, take the medical examination, fill out the paperwork, and receive our instructions. We broke into groups and were sent to our barracks. I was finally able to get some food inside of me, but it tasted funny, unlike the normal food we had onboard.

A bunch of us guys decided to head back to the EMC for some greasy hamburgers. We hoped it was real beef. At this time, I did not care anymore. Five-thirty came early on again the next morning, especially since I do not remember going to sleep the night before. We were back on another train and this time, we headed towards Chuncheon City and Camp Page, in South Korea. This will be my home for the *next year.*

Camp Page is located about fifteen miles from the Demilitarized Zone. Chuncheon had a few nice buildings around the city with some crude housing.
We stayed in the Transient Quarters for five days and then, assigned to my new company. You will be happy to know that I picked up a job at the local cinema. Here is a few bucks to hold you over until next month. Give the children a hug and a kiss from me. One for you too, Rosie. I miss you so much."

Love, Swanny

Norman's letter was a refreshing diversion from my life and I must have read it a hundred times. I kept it tucked under my pillow at night.

Inadvertently, the army lost Norman's pay records before he left. Luckily, Norman sent enough money to pay for the first months' rent, and this left me with $10 to purchase groceries.

Every day I stayed home to care for the children. I cooked, cleaned, and played with them in the back yard. I became acquainted with my neighbors too. However, for some strange reason, Mrs. Meyers seemed to hover over me. By this time, Teri was three years old, Wayne was 20 months old, and Barry was eight months old. When I ran out of money, I resorted to the Red Cross and St. Vincent de Paul's for help until Norman's pay arrived.

St. Vincent de Paul was a blessing in disguise! I told them my circumstances and they helped by providing food and furniture. The priest was so kind and caring, and occasionally he stopped by for a visit. I appreciated how he checked up on us and asked if there was anything, I might need.

I was earning $1.50 an hour babysitting for a German woman across the street. She worked nights and did not return home until midnight. When I babysat, my children were always present with me.

One evening, her baby had a severe case of diarrhea. I did not want to bring the children with me because I was concerned that they may become infected. I left the kids in the apartment sleeping and asked Mrs. Meyers to listen for them while I went to work. Every half-hour, I raced back across the street and checked up on the kids. They were sound asleep. I desperately needed money and it was a good job to have. Adjusting for inflation, $1.50 an hour in 1958 is equal to making $13.75 an hour in today's money! That is why I took the job!

Teri, Wayne, and Barry were taking their afternoon nap, and Madam Butterfly was playing softly on the record player. Exhausted, I fell asleep on the chair in the living room. As a mother's instinct would have it, I made sure to check on them every hour. I woke up disoriented when someone started banging on the front door.

"Mrs. Swanson?" the police officer asked.

"Yes, I am Mrs. Swanson. How may I help you?" I asked.

"Where are your children?" the officer questioned coldly.

"They are in their rooms sleeping. Why are you asking?" I questioned.

Without a moment's hesitation, the two police officers pushed their way inside the apartment, proceeded to the children's room, and grabbed them!

"Why are you taking my children? I have done nothing wrong!" I said, pleading with the officer. "Where are you taking them?" I cried trying to block them from taking the children away.

The officers put my children in the back of their cruiser. One officer interrogated the children while the other questioned me. I think I must have said something to upset him, because he became very angry with me.

"You foreign bitch. Your children are going down to the station with us right now," he said in a condescending voice. "And, you'll never get them back!" he threatened.

At that moment, the officer jumped into the vehicle and drove off. I can still picture the faces of my children peering out the rear window crying.

Frantically, I pulled myself together and headed down to the station. When I arrived, the police told me Teri, Wayne, and Berry were in an orphanage until the hearing. They told me where the children were, and I was able to go to the home with the priest, and bring the children their clothes.

The matriarch of the children's home refused the priest and I from entering the building or seeing the children. She even refused the clothes I brought. I could not check on their condition. She slammed the door in our faces and I cried all the way home.

In court, the judge said that I was unconcerned with the welfare of my children, because I never attempted to see them, or bring them clothes. Thank God, the priest, and the woman from the Red Cross accompanied me to the hearing. They testified, saying that I tried to visit my children, but denied visitation rights. They also told the judge that my home was in immaculate condition. I never left dirty dishes in the sink, and the refrigerator was always full of food. I explained to the judge that the army lost my husband's pay records, and I was babysitting for the neighbor to earn a decent living. That explanation was not good enough for the judge.

The courts did not release the children in my care. I had to seek the assistance of the Red Cross to bring Norman home on an emergency leave from South Korea. If the army had sent Norman's pay, I would have not needed to work.

The following month, Norman and I returned to the courts, with the woman from the Red Cross and the priest. Norman convinced the judge to return the children. For some strange reason, the courts awarded sole custody of the children to Norman. Was it because I was not an American Citizen? Was it because they viewed me as a single mother? I do not know. I never received an explanation. All I knew was that the courts allowed me to take care of the children while Norman was serving in the army in South Korea.

The children were so happy when they saw their father. We were one big happy family again! The next day, I went into labor.

Our Fourth Child is Born – 1959

DADS IN THE delivery room may be routine these days, but not back in the 1950s. Childbirth was an event few American fathers experienced with their wives.

While I lay there in labor, the nurses were busy running in and out of the delivery room. Norman paced back and forth in the 'stork club' while the other fathers puffed nervously on their cigarettes. Norman told me he was close enough to hear me scream out in pain.

In January 1959, our beautiful daughter, Gloria, was born in the Madigan Army Medical Center. The birth of a baby is one of life's most wondrous moments. I watched the doctor clamp, then cut the umbilical cord, raise her upside down, slapping her on her backside. She began to cry. Gloria took her first breath of life. The doctor handed Gloria to the nurse where she immediately wrapped her in a towel, and sucked the fluids from her nose and mouth. The nurse washed the amniotic fluid from her body, placed a knitted hat on top of her head, and handed me my newborn. Joyful tears came to my eyes and Gloria stopped crying. The doctor congratulated me and walked out of the delivery room to tell Norman the good news. Norman walked in and saw me holding Gloria in my arms. His eyes sparkled with deep love and affection. I remained in the hospital for a week before returning home. I was 23 years old and we had four beautiful children, Teri,

Wayne, Barry, and now Gloria.

Before Norman returned to Korea, little Wayne, who was two years old at the time, accidentally hit our newborn over the head with a heavy wooden toy. Gloria's head split open, fracturing her skull. Leaving the children in the care of a neighbor, Norman, and I rushed to the emergency room. The nurses immediately took Gloria into the operating room. Norman held me in his arms as I broke down and cried. Gloria's head was stitched-up and she remained in intensive care for a week. Norman postponed his return to Korea. He reached out to the Red Cross, explained the situation, and asked permission to extend his leave. The Red Cross denied his request, informing him nothing could be done until the following Monday. Norman's ship was leaving on Saturday. Because his love for his children was greater, Norman decided to miss his ship and go AWOL. When Gloria returned from the hospital, Norman handed himself over to the military police. They gave him the choice of either being court-martialed or, he could take a voluntary reduction in pay. This meant he will lose one stripe and his records would remain intact. Norman took the reduction in pay and returned to Korea to fulfill his duty.

After Norman left, I was at home with the children and unemployed. Embarrassed, I returned to the Red Cross and requested additional assistance. Somehow, they arranged with Piggly Wiggly to let me have a twenty-five dollar advance on my grocery bill each month until I could pay them back.

Norman returned from Korea on September 28, 1959. It was so nice to have him home for a change. In January 1960, new orders arrived, and the entire family moved to Ft. Jackson, in Columbia, South Carolina.

From Tacoma to South Carolina – 1960

BY FEBRUARY 1960, the military moved us to Columbia, South Carolina. We rented the upstairs of a two-story house on 1414 St. Anthony's Rd. It was a beautiful brick home with three bedrooms, one bath, on a quarter-acre, nestled among the oak trees. It was large enough to accommodate all of us easily. To the north side of the house, was a large park.

We rented the house from Mrs. Abbar, an Arabic woman who lived downstairs. I had to make sure she took her heart medication every day.

Norman's new assignment was to Headquarters Detachment, in the Third Battalion Training Regiment at Ft. Jackson. He started training to become a Staff Sergeant. Here, he would learn the best leadership and technical skills required to prepare him to lead a squad and platoon-size units.

I was pregnant with our fifth child, Joann. I remember waking up very early one morning to a blackbird sitting at the end of my bed. It terrified me so much that when I moved my feet to scoot it away, it flew around the room instead of out the window.

In a panic, I called the base.

"Is Norman Swanson there?" I asked with a quiver in my voice.

"No. He is busy. Is this an emergency?" the person

asked.

"Yes! This is an emergency! He must come home right away!" I yelled into the phone.

"Alright then. We'll get him out there right away," the voice on the other end of the line said.

I hung up the phone and waited for Norman to arrive. The children were sound asleep in their rooms.

A military vehicle came screeching up the driveway. I could hear Norman running up the stairs. He burst through the door.

"What's the problem? Are you in labor?" he hurriedly asked.

"No. There's a bird in my bedroom and I want it out of here!" I replied.

Immediately, I saw Norman's disposition change. I could tell he was extremely upset with me, but he did not show it. Norman shooed the bird out of the room.

"Now, don't *ever* call me for something like that again!" he ordered pointing his finger at me. I saw he was embarrassed, especially in front of his commanding officer. I never did bother Norman again after that.

Mrs. Abbar was wonderful to have around the house. Our fifth child, Joann was born in June 1960. While I was in the hospital giving birth, Mrs. Abbar stayed home and watched the children. Norman could not take time off to be with me in the hospital when I gave birth. I only saw him in the morning and in the evening.

By July 1961, Norman received orders and the entire family was shipping out to Germany. I was so afraid to tell Mrs. Abbar. I held back on telling her until I found the right time. Since we lived in her house, we became such close friends.

Unexpectedly, Ms. Abbar died. Her son found her dead on the kitchen floor. I believe she had a heart attack. The next day, her son came over and told me we had to leave. We paid the rent until the end of July and I demanded that we stay until the end of the month. Her son made it very difficult for us to live there. He placed items on the stairs, forcing us to walk around them.

Mrs. Abbar's body lay in a coffin in the downstairs living room. The entire family and most of her friends attended to pay their respects. I delicately explained to the children that Mrs. Abbar was no longer with us. Teri cried. She could no longer visit Mrs. Abbar and spend time with her cat. I stayed upstairs with the children the entire time, keeping myself busy, and consoling the children. I heard the family arguing downstairs. They were loud, screaming at each other about the money, and who would inherit the house.

By the end of the month, our belongings were packed. The military sent a truck to move our belongings. We left for Germany on August 1, 1961.

South Carolina to Germany – 1961

WE ARRIVED SAFELY in Germany and set up our new home in a Bavarian village called Bad Tölz. Bad Tölz is beautiful, and tourists flock there for the spas, historic medieval town, and views of the majestic Bavarian Alps. On the western bank of the Isar River, lies Kurverwaltung, a health resort, whose iodine-rich waters soothes and heals the body. Words cannot describe the beauty of this region in Germany.

Norman's post was located at the old SS-Junkerschule, which now houses the U.S. Army 1st Battalion.

I found a babysitter and Norman and I decided to visit the Baroque Cloister Benediktbeuern. Hand in hand, we strolled along the walkways of this beautiful monastery. Beyond the basilica, the monks grew an array of vegetables and herbs. I wanted to walk inside the garden and pick the tomatoes right off the vines.

We stepped inside the chapel. To the right, I noticed there was a glass coffin with an uncannily lifelike visage, clad in nun's robes who reminded me of St. Bernadette of Lourdes. She was beautiful. In the distance, I heard the monks chant and sing. People walked around in silence, admiring the beauty of the architecture, or kneeling to pray. On both sides of the altar, were glass cases, skeletons of the princes of the principalities, dressed in their full regalia.

Monks sold their wine, cheese, and meat to the tourists. We sat at their delightful café and drank a cup of coffee. It was breathtaking. The Alps in the distance, the monks were chanting, the air was crisp, and here I am in Germany with my family.

We stayed in Bad Tölz until February 1962, when Norman transferred to Murnau.

Murnau – 1962

FOR SOME REASON, Norman started drinking. Oh boy, did he enjoy his Griesbräu beer!

I was pregnant with our sixth child and while Norman was at work, I was home taking care of the children. One evening, he did not come home at his usual time. I began to worry. I kept telling myself that he was all right, because nobody from the base called to tell me otherwise. At two o'clock in the morning, I panicked when I heard someone knocking at the door.

"Open up the door sweetheart! This is Woody-Wood Pecker!" he sang in a drunken stupor.

I felt relieved that he was safe and angry at the same time as he was drunk, again. "Go away!" I yelled at him.

He pleaded with me, but I refused to let him into the apartment. I was so angry with him for making me worry unnecessarily. He could have called to let me know he was going out with his friends that evening. How inconsiderate I thought. I finally gave in, and when I opened the door, Norman was standing there with a short Scotsman wearing his Highland dress!

"We've gotten ourselves into a wee bit of a jam, Ma'am," he said, talking in his heavy Scottish accent. "May we come in?"

Norman pushed his way past his new friend, into the living room, and immediately passed out on the couch.

"Well, awa, Norman, and I were stoatin' aboot with the boys, when I suddenly noticed the time. I am sorry to bring 'iem pie-eyed home like this, Ma'am."

The Scotsman looked like a responsible family man and wanted to return to base. However, with the gates locked, they had no place to go except to the apartment. He told me that Norman had 20 Marks on him. Norman was smart. He knew he could not go off base in his military clothes. The Scotsman explained how Norman walked to the PX, and bought himself a pair of pants, a shirt, shoes, and a carry bag for his fatigues. The reason he did not come home was that they were out drinking.

The Scotsman asked if I could help him return to base. With Norman passed out, I accompanied the Scotsman back to the garrison. When we arrived at the gate, the Scotsman asked me to bend over, explaining to me that he would climb on my back to jump over the fence. When he grabbed the top of the fence and pulled himself over, I looked up, and that is when I found out that Scotsmen wear underwear under their kilts!

In April 1963, our sixth child, Gunard was born. We then relocated to Garmisch-Partenkirchen.

Garmisch-Partenkirchen - 1963

NORMAN'S NEXT ASSIGNMENT was to Headquarters Company, Co. A, in the United States Army Europe. The USAREUR is the Army Service Component Command/Theater Army, responsible for directing United States Army operations throughout the U.S. European Command Area of Responsibility. By this time, the Soviets had closed the border crossing points and built the Berlin Wall, isolating the western sector of the city from East Germany and the Soviet sector, East Berlin. The crisis cooled in Berlin from 1962 to 1963, and augmenting forces returned to the United States. I believe Norman's assignment to this area was to relieve the troops who returned home.

We lived in the Breitenau Housing Area adjacent to the Artillery Kaserne. This close-knit military community consisted of service and civilian family members. Our apartment was furnished and stocked with furniture, linens, and tableware. Seven bedrooms, three bathrooms with three individual toilet rooms called Klosett's, a large kitchen, and a living room, gave us enough room to move freely about. The military supplied us with our food until we were able to do our grocery shopping.

A long hallway connected the apartments. The

floors were so highly polished that you could see your reflection in them. Using rags, the kids slid up and down the hallway, and acted as if it was their very own playground.

In 1936, Garmisch hosted the Winter Olympics. I saw the ski jump from our apartment window. Just minutes away was King Ludwig II's castle Schloss Neuschwanstein, and Munich was a short ride to the north.

The Garmisch Family Morale Welfare and Recreation program (GFMWR) helped us move, provided our supplies, and arranged for babysitting services. By this time Teri was eight years old, Wayne was six, Barry was five, Gloria was four, Joann was three, and Gunard was newly born. The kids attended the Garmisch Elementary school while I stayed home to watch Joann and Gunard.

One evening, I secured babysitting services for the kids so that Norman and I could spend some time together. We heard the Hofbräuhaus was an authentic place to dine. I ordered hot cucumber soup and a side salad. I nearly fell off my bench when the waiter served the entrée. The veal cutlet, garnished with lemon and a sprig of parsley, hung over the sides of the plate! The ambiance was delightful. We sat at long wooden tables with the tourists and locals, some who dressed in their traditional Bavarian attire. When the Oom-Pah Pah band started playing, people locked arms, and sang. We rocked back and forth in time to the music. Everyone was having such a wonderful time!

When the folk dancers started performing, they made Norman, and I get up and dance. I was so shy at that time and they would not take 'no' for an answer. One of the men grabbed me. I did not know the steps, but that did not matter. He was considerate of my awkwardness.

On another date, Norman suggested we join the locals at the ice park. Norman loved to ice skate and I could not. One of his friends suggested we go to the Riessersee, a little lake nestled between the forest, and the Bavarian Alps. All bundled up, I put my skates on and Norman gently eased me onto the ice. I fell on my butt so many times. We laughed and had a chuffed time. It was so beautiful being outside skating on the lake with the Bavarian Alps in the distance. It was magical and beautiful.

One of our neighbors recommended we visit the Old Parish Church of St. Martin built in 1280 A.D. We obtained the keys from the Hofbräuhaus. How I admire the Germans for preserving their history. There were several lavish gothic mural paintings inside the parish, and the beautiful stained-glass windows were awe-inspiring. Equally impressive, was the 23-foot high representation of St. Christopher from the year 1330, as well as the Baroque-style high altar. This small parish can hold 30 – 40 people.

Norman spoke fluent German, which made it easy for us when we went shopping. We enjoyed strolling on

Ludwigstrasse and looking in at the store's displays. The shops were beautiful, pristine and clean. Everything sparkled and shined. Picturesque little alleys from antique stores, to established traditional bakeries, bustled with locals and tourists. The owners were friendly, accommodating, and the experience was relaxing. Lined along the narrow streets are historic buildings in the Bavarian Gasthaus style: three or four floors, swept open dark-brown wooden shutters, and street-facing facades painted in pastel-hued imagery of religious, pastoral and regional scenes. *And,* the flowers! There were so many flowers everywhere! I especially loved seeing the geraniums with their trailing ivy vines hanging from the balconies. Never in my life had I seen such large baskets of petunias either! I felt welcomed here. Everything was so decorative and the residents took pride in the beauty of their town.

One day, while Norman was working at the base, I decided to take the children for a hike. We walked on the Ferchensee-Lautersee Loop. We started our hike from Adolf-Baader Strasse, and continued on the path into the meadows, and up the hillside. My impressionable budding sense of imagination was blossoming with magical legends of alpine dwarfs, trolls, and princesses who found their prince charming. Hiking in the surrounding area is an activity enjoyed by the locals and I can see why. Spending time with my family in this area brought us closer together. I pushed Gunard in the stroller as the kids skipped along the path exploring the flowers, bugs, and the other little things along the way.

The Bavarian Alps are part of the Northern Limestone Alps in southeastern Germany. They extend from the Rhine valley in Vorarlberg, Austria in the west, along the border between Bavaria and Tyrol, through Salzburg, finally ending in Wienerwald in the city of Vienna. The highest peak is the Zugspitze, 9,718 feet above sea level. It has two glaciers that people explore both in the summer and ski on during the winter months. On this hike, we walked along the Kreuzeck Mountains.

The double-red and white painted striped marker on the post signified the path to take, leading us from the village to the open meadows, around the lakes of Ferchensee and Lautersee, and then back to Garmisch.

Herds of grazing goats spread out across the meadow. Some relaxed on the ground enjoying the warm sun as the 'kids' frolicked around them. Others stood, and chewed their cud, content in their peaceful surroundings. The continuous clanging of the bell marked the leader of this herd.

The majestic cut-glass peaks of the Alps, and the fragrant emerald meadows trimmed by a pastel carpet of gold clover, milk kraut, daisies, and bellflowers, compliment God's beautiful landscape. I felt a sense of spirituality being here.

We followed the trail until we came to a signpost pointing us in the direction of Ferchensee. This meandering trail continued through the deciduous forest. The steep acclivity did not dampen our spirits. We were having fun hanging on to each other's shirts, walking up the trail, making a game out of it. We must have been a sight in the eyes of the locals.

We entered into an area of dense woods. The delightful scent of pine filled the air and the area was absent of undergrowth. Little sunlight penetrated onto the ground.

Barry was the mischievous one in the family, and loved to explore. He walked close to the side of the ridge and fell over. Luckily, he grabbed a branch and held onto it for dear life. The German Boy Scouts heard the commotion and came running over. They saw what had happened and rescued him out of the tree.

"Thank you! I don't know what I would have done if you were not here," I said in gratitude.

"It is not a good idea for you to take him up this mountain," the leader of the troop said. Then, off they trotted on their way.

Teri noticed a clump of large trumpet-shaped flowers with an intense blue hue and started picking them. One of the local hikers noticed this and compassionately asked her in German not to pick the flowers because folklore says, if you pick the Spring Gentians, someone will die.

The views unfolded along the trail to Ferchensee and they are magnificent. We rounded the corner and came upon the picturesque lake of Ferchensee. It was so peaceful and idyllic. One of the mountains waved hello to us from behind the pine trees. I wished Norman were there to see this. It was practically dark when we returned to our humble abode. Norman was waiting for us wondering where we were the entire day!

Sometimes, Norman and I drove up the mountains and walked the trails, catching views of the beautiful white edelweiss naturally growing on the cliffs. I loved our romantic walks. We held hands, took in the scenery, and talked about how blessed we are to be living in Germany. The snowcapped Alps were around us. The sky was a deep shade of blue, and the beautiful green meadows dotted with wild yellow flowers grew in the fields. It was so beautiful. I could not get over how crisp the air was.

I remember seeing goats grazing on the mountainside. It reminded me of England. Sometimes, when I lay myself down to sleep, I think back upon those days, and dream about what a wonderful time we had in Germany. I can still hear Norman's voice in my head telling me how much he loves me. It was very romantic and we were both very much in love.

Norman enjoyed going to the NCO club to dance. He was an exceptional dancer. Many times, he would bring me onto the floor and try to teach me how to dance the Polka. It is a fast-paced 2/4 dance step with a preparatory hop, followed by a chassé, step-together-step dance movement, done with the left foot first, and then with the right foot. After the evening at the club, he escorted me home before leaving again. He told me that he had to 'run out' for a little bit. He was so sweet about it. I did not think much about where he was going or what he was going to do. I let him go on his way and trusted that he would return shortly. After waiting an hour for him, I went to bed.

When he was what you call "buzzed," he would be everyone's friend. It upset me the most when he started buying everyone at the NCO club rounds of drinks. When he was drunk, he only thought about himself, and not the financial responsibility he had towards his family. I knew I had to put my foot down and make a stand. The climax came on one particular afternoon, when he came home from the base, and asked if I would mind if he went out with his friends for a drink. Please do not get me wrong. I loved Norman dearly. However, his drinking was getting out of hand, and it was hurting the family financially, and hurting me, emotionally.

"Are you going out to drink?" I asked.

"I'll probably have a few with the guys," he replied.

"If you want to, go ahead. I am not going to stop you. This is the end of it Norman. I am going to leave you," I responded in a stern voice.

"What?" he exclaimed.

"You heard me. I am leaving you," I said.

"Oh, please don't go Dorothy" he pleaded, getting on his knees. "I swear I will never touch another drop of alcohol ever again."

"I am leaving you Norman," I threatened. We started arguing. This was our first fight.

"Well, you are not going to take the children," he demanded.

"You can have them!" I remarked. I did not mean it. I wanted the children, but I did not know what else to do to get Norman to stop drinking. He was out of control. He was gone every night drinking at the club, and I had no money to buy food or clothes for the children. I had to threaten him to get him to realize the seriousness of the situation.

I think deep down inside, Norman realized that his drinking was creating a problem in our marriage, because he listened to my concerns and agreed with me. From that moment on, he never went out drinking with his friends. He switched from beer to diet coke and never touched another drop of alcohol. Norman kept his word. On the other hand, my sister, Gloria, tried so many times to get Norman to start drinking again, especially during the holidays. I was very proud of Norman, standing up to my sister's pressure. He never backed down. Norman knew if he ever started drinking again, I would keep my word and leave.

Norman and I were so happy when our seventh beautiful child, Marcella, was born in September 1964 in Munich, Germany.

Goodbye Germany – 1964

IN NOVEMBER 1964, Norman received orders to return to the United States. His reassignment took him to HHD 90th Replacement Battalion, Company E, ISB, TSB, and the family to Ft. Benning, GA.[9]

By this time, Norman had received his WWII Victory, Good Conduct, and Carbine Marksman medals, in addition to receiving his honorable service lapel pin, colloquially called the Ruptured Duck, three bronze Good Conduct loops, his Marksman Rifle medal, and his fourth bronze Good Conduct Medal. His military rank became Staff Sergeant/Specialist 6 (E-6), and he was the squad leader in his new company.

As our time in Germany was ending, we packed, and organized the apartment for inspection. The military was strict and everything had to be in total compliance with our lease. All was in order except for the dust found on top of the refrigerator motor, and the wax build-up on the floors. We failed the first inspection. The inspector told us that we had to hire their house cleaners, and pay $25.00, to pass the next inspection. Instead of paying the house cleaners, I decided to save the money and I would clean the dust

---

[9] Headquarters and Headquarters Detachment, Intermediate Staging Base, Training Support Battalions

from the refrigerator motor, and remove the excess wax from the floors. I had a difficult time removing the excess wax because it was too much work for me to do by myself. I did my best and hoped the floors would pass inspection. I noticed the kitchen bench looked dull, and I polished it. The inspector returned, and approved the refrigerator, but not the floors. He sat down on the kitchen bench and began explaining to us that we had to hire their house cleaners if we wanted to pass inspection. Reluctantly we agreed.

The inspector stood up, shook Norman's hand, and turned to leave. Norman's eyes bulged out of his head! I forgot to wipe the excess polish off the bench and the inspector had a brown stain mark around his buttock. We looked at each other and giggled.

The GFMWR assisted us in the move to Georgia. We left Garmisch by bus and traveled to Munich to catch our flight.

On the tarmac sat a Douglas C-124 Globemaster military cargo and transport plane that flew us directly to Georgia. Boy that was a big plane!

We walked up the ramp into the twin door opening located underneath the flight deck and took our seats. A big old army tank sat right in front of us. We were the only passengers, besides the crew, on the flight.

For such a long flight, the cloth seats became uncomfortable. Four propeller engines roared through the nine-hour long trip. The kids were exhausted and fell asleep right away. I could not sleep. Daylight shined the entire flight home. A member of the crew gave each of us a little box lunch before arriving in Georgia.

Norman never spoke in detail about his duties, but he did tell me that he hated his new assignment to the Intermediate Staging Base Training Support Battalion. I stayed home to watch the kids.

In April 1966, Chris was born. Now, we had eight children. Teri is 10, Wayne is nine, Barry is eight, Gloria is seven, Joann is five, Gunard is three, and Marcella is a year and a half old. The kids attended elementary school, and I hired a babysitter to take care of Gunard, Marcella, and Chris, while I searched for a job. Ft. Benning had no nursing positions available. I decided to use my experience as a server and found work at an upscale British Restaurant called "Dunnigan's Beef House." So many celebrities ate there. Sonny & Cher, John Wayne, and Milton Berle were some of the autographed photos that hung on the walls. Mr. Dunnigan was the owner and we all called him Mr. D.

At first, Mr. D and I worked well together. After a while, people thought we were married because we argued all the time. I would tell him straight out when I disagreed with him about how he prepared his meals or how he treated the other employees. On many occasions, I threatened to leave.

The Beef House used Wilton Armetale Tankard Beer Steins when serving their beer. When they are highly polished, they look almost like silver mugs.

Every time someone stole one of the mugs, I had to pay for the replacement out from my tips. I argued with Mr. D about having to pay for the loss of his mugs. I did not think it was fair to me, especially when I knew I returned every stein to the kitchen. He insisted I pay and that is when I quit without giving notice.

I found employment at the Ralston Hotel in Columbus, Ga. Mr. D came to the hotel every day and begged me to return to his restaurant. He told me I was the most professional employee he had, and many patrons wanted me back. I always replied with a resounding "NO!" I was surprised when he returned to the hotel dressed in his finest attire. On my break, he spoke with such charisma. It reminded me of when I first started working for him. He agreed to give me a small raise and I agreed to return to his restaurant. I handed in my notice, and two weeks later, I left the Ralston Hotel, and returned to work at the Beef House.

To be honest with you, I think it may have been a love/hate relationship. Even though I was married, I looked at him as a good friend. He never tried to put hands on me, because I was older and had children. I felt sorry for his wife though, because she was a wonderful person, and she was very nice to my family and me. Mrs. D gave me all her hand-me-downs for the children. She was a caring and compassionate woman.

Shortly after returning to work, Mr. D's shenanigans started again. I noticed him wash the hair off from the steak and put lemon juice on it! It reminded me how Uncle Alf prepared his meat. I knew that was not a normal way to prepare the steak before serving it to the customer. I did not like it when he looked at the patrons and remarked sarcastically, "look at those people eat that! They love it!"

Mr. D hired a black adolescent boy to wash the dishes. When the boy asked for his pay, Mr. D chased him out of the kitchen with a fork, and pushed him into the cooler. Mr. D slammed the door tight and yelled, "cool off in there boy!"

"You can't do that!" I yelled at Mr. D, begging him to release the boy.

"I can do anything I want to do. This is my restaurant, Rosie. Now, go away!" he said pushing me aside.

Eventually, he let the young man out of the cooler. I saw him run out the back door. Poor kid, I thought. He never received his wages, either.

Another time, I saw the chef cut off the tip of his finger, and it fell right into the pot with the corn beef. Mr. D told us "not to waste it - it will be fine!" Mr. D only served corn beef to his employees. I was very reluctant to eat the meal that day. I had a bad feeling about the sandwich. Wouldn't you know it! I bit right into the tip of the chef's finger! I screamed and spat it out onto the floor.

"What's wrong with you?" Mr. D asked.

"I just ate the chef's finger!" I screamed.

"Oh, you're just imagining it!" he replied.

That was the last time I saw the tip of the finger, and that was the last time I ate his corn beef.

One of the benefits of working at the Beef House was that Mr. D allowed me to bring the kids in for meals. He allowed them to eat the small hamburger patties, while Norman and I could eat a full meal. The kids ate free while Norman and I paid the employee-discounted price.

One of the chefs befriended me. He was kind to me. I do not remember his name, but I do remember that he was single and a confirmed bachelor. He invited the family to his farm located over the bridge in Alabama. He had three beautiful white British Alsatians.

For part of the year, the chef would go out on the road with his traveling fair. He owned the balloon booth and that is how he made extra income. I never understood the arrangement Mr. D had with him because he was away during the season and returned in the fall to resume his work.

I noticed Mr. D liked to hire the young, good-looking girls to work as servers. He hired them even though they had no prior experience. I felt something peculiar when Mr. D told me that I did not have to close up the restaurant one evening. He asked the new girl instead. I knew what he wanted. I tried to warn her, but she did not listen to me. The next day, I confronted him and he denied the allegations of having sex with her.

I heard from one of the employees that Mr. D had a dishonorable discharge from the service and married his wife because her family was wealthy. Whether or not it was true, I do not know. However, I do admit he was handsome.

I enjoyed serving the Jewish family that came in after their service. I grew to know them, their likes and dislikes. They tipped me very well. I do not know how Mr. D found out about the large tips I received from them. He told me I could not serve them anymore unless I shared my 'wealth' with everyone else. When Mr. D assigned another server to the group, they were displeased with her, and told Mr. D that they only wanted me to serve them. I was so happy the following week when they returned. I thanked each one of them.

When Norman came to pick me up from work, I showed him my tips. Sometimes I had over one-hundred dollars in one night!

I was paid $10.00 a week in salary plus tips. I worked the evening schedule because the tips were better. I was upset when Mr. D told us we had to share our tips. I was good at my job and I know I always made more in tips than everyone else did. I thought it was unfair for me to share my tips, so I decided to hold back.

I loved it when a family came into the restaurant. I knew the wife held the purse strings. The other girls did not want to serve the families. Instead, they wanted to serve the big parties or the group of executives.

I thought it was strange when I received a $10.00 tip for serving a piece of cherry cheesecake and coffee to a male customer! He asked me to sit down and converse with him. He offered me a cup of coffee. I told him that I cannot sit with customers and that I can drink all the free coffee I want. He left and I never saw him again. He was quite good looking though, but I knew what he wanted!

Returning to Germany – 1967

IN 1967, THE entire family returned to Murnau, Germany. Murnau is a market town in the district of Garmisch-Partenkirchen, in the Oberbayern region of Bavaria, Germany. Norman's transfer took him to Kimbro Kaserne, the United States Army Engineer Ordinance School. The property sits on 400 acres and is named posthumously in honor of Technician Fourth Grade Truman Kimbro Company C, 2nd Engineer Combat Battalion, 2nd Infantry Division. The school accommodates the heavy artillery, special weapons, and military police units, including the Engineer, Ordnance, Logistics, and Executive and Career Development Departments, with its Headquarters in Oberammergau. Twenty-two short years ago, we were fighting the Germans in WW II. Today, the army is collaborating and training the German Army at Kimbro.

The latest weapons coupled with his fighting skills, the American soldier stands ready, always on the alert, to defend the United States and the American people against aggression. One problem confronting modern military organizations is the maintenance and proper balance of trained specialists among the troops. USAEUR maintains several army schools in Europe.

Since 1947, the home of the United States Army Reserve Europe Engineer School trained enough personnel to meet the requirements for which experts are not readily available. The changeover of personnel constantly leads to the need for new technicians. While the army may need an equipment operator in England, they may need a welder in France. Kimbro Kaserne is where the soldiers train. The emphasis is hands-on learning, whether it be operating heavy equipment, demolition, ordinance, or rebuilding, the army always has trained personnel available. Classes were small, with four to eight trainees receiving personalized attention for their designated skills. To an army man, the engineer usually calls forth thoughts of one of the most delicate of operations in modern warfare – the use of mines, demolition charges, and booby traps. The bulk of the courses at the Murnau School were constructive rather than destructive. An army engineer not only needs to learn how to blow things up, but he must also learn how to put them back together again. Norman taught classes but he did not tell me specifically what he was teaching.

It was a beautiful spring morning when Norman left for his dentist appointment. He kissed me on the cheek, wished me a good day, and headed out the door. I prepared breakfast for the children and got them ready for school. Marcella and Chris were in the living room playing. I was washing the dishes, looking out the window, and heard the birds chirping. Military mothers with their babies in strollers sat on the bench talking to one another. The flowers were in full bloom. In the distance, I saw the familiar snow-capped Bavarian Alps. I felt so at home and blessed, knowing my family and I were in this beautiful part of God's world again.

As I completed my morning chores, the doorbell rang. It was a military officer and he urged me to go with him right away. Norman was in the hospital dying. I grabbed my purse, ran to the next apartment, and asked one of the mothers to watch over the kids for me. The officer drove us to the Munich hospital, an hour away, and in the car, he explained what happened.

The dentist gave Norman a shot of Novocaine and he immediately went into cardiac arrest. The dentist thought Norman had only fainted and started waving a cloth over his face. A medic happened to walk by and recognized Norman's condition. He immediately gave him CPR and called for the medics.

I raced into intensive care and saw Norman hooked up to the oxygen concentrator. His complexion was pale. The Chaplin stood over him, giving Norman his last rights. I held Norman's hand and told him how much I loved him. I arranged to secure babysitting services for the children while I remained in the hospital with Norman until he fully recuperated.

Norman received temporary disability because the army thought he would improve. He did not. Norman was never the same again.

Georgia to Kentucky – 1967

IN THE LATE summer of 1967, the entire family returned to Ft. Benning, Georgia. We moved into the military housing on base so that Norman can receive the medical treatment he so desperately needed. I resumed my evening shift at Dunnigan's Beef House.

During the day, I was at home watching the kids. Sometimes, out of sheer exhaustion, I fell asleep on the couch and Norman was supposed to watch the children. He was on disability. He was not watching the children that day, as he should have been. The kids came up with the brilliant idea to use the mattress and slide out the bedroom window!

The neighbors saw what happened and called Family Advocacy. That evening, I received a call at work. It was a woman from protective services telling me to return home right away.

When I arrived, a woman from Family Advocacy was asking the children questions. I became nervous and thought I was going to lose them again. After they left, I called my friend, Edith, in Louisville, KY., and explained what happened. She told me to come over right away with Norman, and the children. I gave my notice at Dunnigan's and Norman arranged for us to leave the base. Within three weeks, we packed our clothes and drove to Kentucky.

Our entire family moved into Edith's three-bedroom home, along with her husband, and three children. Edith was a full-blooded Cherokee Indian and her husband was a full-blooded Black Foot Indian. They made their wealth by owning and managing rental properties.

Norman and I slept in one of the children's rooms as our children slept on the floor throughout the house. The next day, Norman and I purchased bunk beds for the kids.

Edith was a kind and compassionate woman. Not once did she become upset with the children or at us for moving into her home. We lived in Edith's home for about a month. I helped her in the kitchen, with the laundry, and kept the house neat and clean. Norman and Edith's husband searched for a new automobile and a home for us.

Let me tell you, cooking for fifteen mouths is not an easy task. One evening, we served a spaghetti dinner with whole tomatoes instead of sauce. My children were not accustomed to eating spaghetti in this manner. I reprimanded the children and told them that if they did not eat what was on their plate, they would go hungry. Believe me, from then on, they ate everything!

Edith was knowledgeable about real estate and she co-signed the loan to help us get our new home on Iron Horse Way. It was a beautiful, large, two-story brick home, with a manicured lawn.

We planted a vegetable garden in the back yard with corn, green beans, peas, tomatoes, and potatoes.

For some reason, the neighbors became angry with us. The homeowners association oversaw the subdivision, and it was in the bylaws that we could not grow corn. We removed the corn patch and kept the vegetable garden intact.

We became good friends with Mr. Willheight, who owned the farm behind us. He asked the boys to watch over his cattle, and to make sure they never crossed the railroad tracks. A few times, I had to call the boys home from school to round-up the cows.

Mr. Willheight gave Teri one of his prized Black Angus cows. She could fatten him up, and by the end of the year, he would take it to the market for butchering.

Mr. Willheight noticed we were always short on food. He gave us, instead of his hogs, his day-old raisin bread and croissants.

The army reassigned Norman, who was still on temporary disability, to report to the Ireland Army Clinic in Ft. Knox, Ky. This is when he started to gamble. He continually lost his winnings, along with his disability income. Because of Norman's gambling addiction, we started having financial difficulties, and could not pay the bills.

The city turned off our water. Luckily, I listened to my intuition and saved the milk containers. I stored them in the basement. Every morning, I walked to the gas station, filled the jugs with water, and brought them back to the house. Each child received one gallon of water a day to bathe in. This is how we survived.

I found enough loose change around the house and in the car, to pay for the water bill, and have it turned back on. Every day, I was home watching the children, and Norman was out gambling. We constantly argued over the bills. I thought he agreed to pay the bills, but he did not.

The next month, an employee from the water department came over, and tried to turn the water off again! I was so angry! I was angry with Norman, and I was angry at the city. I went outside, sat right down on top of the water meter, and I did not move! I argued with the employee, and explained to him that Norman was disabled, and that we had no money to pay for this month's bill. During the middle of my argument, it started snowing heavily. The employee did not care and he called the police. An officer arrived and told me I had to move off the meter. I refused. Crying, I explained the situation again to the police officer. Do you know what the officer said to me? I either move or go to jail. Tears streamed down my face. The police helped me stand, escorted me back to the house, and the city employee shut off our water.

"Not to worry Mrs. Swanson. We'll figure something out," the police officer compassionately said before he left.

The next morning I had the shock of my life! The same police officer returned to the house and he told me that he collected enough money from everyone at the station to pay off our entire water bill! Within the hour, we had water again. That was a lifesaver, until LG&E turned off our electricity.

It was in the deep of winter. Without any notice, I was standing in the kitchen cooking, when all the lights went out. Again, Norman did not pay the bill! I became furious! My mind raced and I was thinking, "What am I going to do now?" Norman was not at home and the kids were at school. Chris was in diapers. "How am I going to heat the house and cook dinner? Norman has the car and there is no way I can get a hold of him. I have no money to pay the electric bill. What am I going to do? This house will have heat, and I will cook dinner tonight, but how?" Then, I remembered we had a fireplace.

When the kids came home from school, they noticed there was no electricity. They could not understand why I was boiling a pot of water on the fireplace. I was making myself a cup of tea. Confused, the children started crying, mostly because they could not watch television. I settled the children around the fireplace and explained the situation. Norman walked into the house and asked what was happening.

"We have no electricity and I had to chop up one of the kid's bedroom sets, and use it to make a fire," I calmly said, sipping on my tea, holding back my anger.

An intense argument ensued in front of the children. I sent them outside to collect firewood. When they returned, Norman and I had settled the argument, and the family pretended we were outside, camping.

We roasted hotdogs and marshmallows. We used the icicles that hung from the eaves to keep our food cold in the refrigerator. The family survived like this for a couple of days. It was most difficult in the middle of the night when the house became cold. I had to get up, clean out the fireplace, and start a new fire before anyone awoke.

Help arrived in the form of the Cancer Society. I had contacted them earlier and requested assistance. Not only did they pay our electric bill for the month, they came over with boxes full of clothes and groceries, a twenty-pound turkey, and make-up for Teri! The kids started crying. I was grateful for the assistance. However, the gambling did not stop there.

Norman continued to gamble and we became further in debt. Sears and JC Penny knocked on the door demanding payments. Out of desperation, I found a babysitter for Chris, and I started looking for a job.

I spoke with the owner of Paquin. He agreed to teach me how to drive and help me obtain my driver's license. Within a week, I was delivering cars for Paquin from his property, in Louisville, across the river into Indiana. With each car I delivered, I was paid $15.00 in cash.

I saved every penny I got my hands on. I did not tell Norman how much money I was making. When the Social Security disability check arrived, I took it to the bank, and cashed it right away. When the bank asked when they were going to receive their mortgage payment, I told them 'soon.' When the debt collectors showed up at the front door, I told them we had no money. We were on the brink of bankruptcy. The only way out of this horrible situation was to return to England. Norman agreed. By this time, he was retired.

To raise the money we needed for our flight to England, I sold the freezer, the refrigerator, and all the furniture. We packed up the car, and drove to New York City, leaving our first little home behind!

Kentucky to England – 1972

EIGHT KIDS, a mutt Teri picked up at a rest stop, and a little white Ford Falcon with two adults, drove non-stop, twelve hours from Louisville, KY to John F. Kennedy Airport in Queens, New York. Realizing we could not take the dog with us, we left it with some people at the next rest stop.

Davis Airlines was not flying on that day. Their terminal was in the Eastern Airlines building and we were told the next flight out would be in four days. For two days, we sat and waited in the arcade railway-looking terminal. Underfoot, the vibrations of the diesel tugs and cart baggage-trains rattled.

An agent from Eastern Airlines approached and questioned why we were sitting in the terminal. Norman did not say a word. I started crying, explaining that someone stole my husband's wallet, and that we had no money. It was not all a lie. All the money we received from the sale of our items paid for our plane tickets to England. We had no money. The agent asked us to remain in the terminal until she returned.

Unbeknownst to us, the agent called the President of Eastern Airlines. When she returned, she told us that Mr. Rickenbacker said to give each one of us a passenger pack containing a toothbrush, toothpaste, and a comb. He even offered to take us by limousine, to the St. George's Hotel in Queens, the same hotel we stayed in when we first arrived in America with our daughter Teri.

The hotel has a long history. It provided lodging for military troops and their families' en-route to or returning from military assignments. We were a military family and that is how we came to stay at the St. George.

For two days, the kids were in their glory, and felt like royalty! They ordered room service, jumped up and down on the beds, and constantly changed the channel on the television set.

Once the opulent destination for such celebrities as F. Scott Fitzgerald, Johnny Weissmuller, the Olympic swimmer and star of the Tarzan movies, and others who ventured over the East River to dine at the hotel's restaurant, the children made this building their playground. Exploring this grand, historic icon, they ventured into the ballroom, took in the Manhattan skyline from the rooftop terrace, and rode up and down in the elevators, evading the staff at every turn.

The next morning, an employee from Davis Airlines picked us up, and drove us to JFK International Airport. As we left the hotel, Norman asked me why I lied to the airline agent. "What else was I going to say to them? We came here without any money. What was I supposed to do?" I replied.

"You should've called your sister and asked her for the money instead," he commented.

I disagreed with him.

We boarded British Caledonian, a private, independent British airline, and took our seats. After I sat down, a man sitting next to me said, "What did you do? Did you rent this airplane?" He could not believe we had eight children flying with us! I was so happy to be returning home.

On the flight to England, I thought about Edith. How disappointed she must have been with us. I felt so guilty for leaving without telling her. I placed the house keys and a note on the kitchen table. I never said goodbye. When we arrived in England, I found the first phone, and called her. I profusely apologized to her for leaving so abruptly. She forgave us and told me that she had rented the house. There was no loss on her part. Once we settled in, I contacted her so she knew where to mail the documents. Norman and I agreed to sign the house 100% over to her.

She is in heaven today. God bless her. She was such an angel.

Finally in England – 1972

WE ARRIVED AT the International Stansted Airport in Stansted Mountfitchet, 42 miles northeast of Central London. My sister, Gloria, met us at the airport. Our disheveled appearance embarrassed her, especially the brown paper bags we carried that held our clothes. Back then, you did not fly without looking like a Hollywood movie star! To Gloria, we looked like a family of vagabonds.

At this time, I had no idea of the difficulties I would encounter with my sister, and her husband, Terry. The problem began with the amount of money Norman received from his military pension. According to my sister's standards, we were rich. She came up with the idea and convinced us to go into the foodservice business with her, and her husband.

Norman purchased the food truck. Gloria used our money to set up the business, secure the licenses, and purchase the supplies. Gloria hired Wayne, a man she knew, to cook and make the sandwiches. Gloria and I served the meals to the construction workers.

All was going well for the first couple of months. We accommodated Gloria's family the best we could. Norman and I purchased bunk beds for our children, and paid for their school uniforms. We paid Gloria's utility bills, telephone, and the groceries.

When life began to feel cramped, Norman and I

thought it would be best to rent a place of our own. Uncle Alf resumed The 46th Café, and established enough credit to co-sign our lease. Norman remained at the café while I left to tell Gloria the good news. She became belligerent and hostile. I ran from her house in tears, leaving the children behind. I returned to the café and told Norman and my uncle what happened. Gloria burst through the door with the children.

"How could you do that to me?" she yelled in front of the patrons. "You don't even know Uncle Alf and Aunt Rose anymore and you are leaving! How dare you!" she screamed. She dropped off the kids and left. The café became silent and the people stared at us.

"You've got to leave Rosie. I cannot take it with Gloria anymore. She has been our only niece since you left 16 years ago to go to America. We do not know you anymore. Alfie signed the papers and you will have no excuse to come back here. You and Norman will now have a place of your own," Aunt Rose reciprocated.

I could not return to Gloria's house that evening. Norman, the kids and I, spent the night at Uncle Alf and Aunt Rose's house. The next morning, I returned to Gloria's house, hoping she had calmed down. I did not want to fight with my sister. I wanted it to be as when we first arrived in England.

I did not expect to see what I found when I returned to Gloria's house. In the middle of her front yard, I saw a large pile of debris. When I walked closer, I noticed it was our mattresses, pillows, the children's clothing, shredded into a heaping pile. I immediately called the police. Two Bobbies arrived, and spoke individually with Gloria, and myself. This was a family dispute and they could do nothing about it. Unfortunately, our new home would not be ready until the following day. We spent one more night at Gloria's house. It was a horrible experience. Gloria walked around the house, slamming cabinet doors, and throwing things in the kitchen. She was arguing with Terry and that scared the children. Terry burst through our bedroom door with such force and anger. He demanded I return the food truck keys to him. I complied. He screamed at me, telling me I was not a partner with Gloria anymore, and told us we had to leave the house immediately. We argued. I told him we would leave first thing in the morning. He slammed the door behind him. I did not sleep at all that evening.

The next morning, Norman, the children, and I, gathered our belongings, and climbed into a black cab. Gloria and Terry did not say a word as we left. Before getting into the cab, I looked back. Terry stood there next to his wife, with his arms crossed, overlooking the pile of debris in their front yard.

It was not until a few months later that a Bobbie came knocking at our door, asking about my sister. It turns out that they found her sitting on the side of the motorway in a confused state of mind.[10] They wanted to know more about the money they found on the ground

---

[10] Motorway is a highway

around her. I informed them that Norman and I used to own a food truck with her, and that Wayne was her employee. The police told me that she took the money from the register and left Wayne alone in the truck. She claimed to have had a nervous breakdown. Gloria blamed me for her nervous breakdown and financial problems. She told the police that I was supporting her and her family, which we were when we lived with her, but at this time, not.

Aunt Rose told me that Gloria and Terry had gone bankrupt. Instead of paying their bills, they saved their money so that they could move to Canada. The bank repossessed the house and the food truck. I did not have the heart to tell Aunt Rose what a difficult time I was having with Norman's gambling. Norman had stopped paying the bills again and we found ourselves terribly in debt, again.

In England, if you do not pay your bills, the collector sends a truck with the words 'DEADBEATS' written in giant letters on the side. This is what Norman and I woke up to one morning. I was so embarrassed. All our neighbors saw the truck parked in front of our house. I told Norman we had to return to the states. We were so heavily in debt.

Because Norman was a veteran, he was able to secure complimentary tickets on a military transport for our return trip back to the States. Two days later, we left everything behind for America.

Norman did not want to leave. Once again, we had

our little suitcases packed, and had to wait two days for a flight back to Georgia. I remember Norman saying that he was never going to return to England. He asked me if I was sure that I wanted to return to the States. I told Norman that Uncle Alf and Aunt Rosie knew we were leaving. We had one week left on our lease, and Uncle Alf was going to pay for it.

I never realized the truth when Norman said, "I'll never go back to England." I have a picture in my mind of him sitting on the suitcase. He looked so sad. He did not want to return to America. He was happy in England.

Father Seriously Ill – 1972

IT IS PAINFUL for me to discuss this part of my life. I received a letter from Gloria informing me that our father had acute leukemia. Her words were urgent, telling me to come to England right away. My sister picked me up at the airport. I felt awkward seeing her under these circumstances, because she pretended everything was acceptable from when we last saw each other. My intuition told me otherwise. I stayed in my parent's house in Milton Keynes. My time in England would be short and I needed to make the most of it.

Every day, I visited my father in the hospital. I held his hand as he explained to me, how the doctor performed a spinal tap, and found leukemia cells in the cerebrospinal fluid. The infusion machine attached to the drip stand, pumped fluids through a central line, releasing a controlled amount of chemotherapy into his body. The ventilator pumped oxygen through slender tubes into his nose, as the monitor beeped rhythmically in time with his heartbeat, showing his vital signs. The greatest challenge I experienced was rebuilding our relationship before he passed away. We reminisced about his performances at the Garrick Theatre, my stubbornness of wanting an education, and seeking his approval, and resentment from him being emotionally unavailable to me when I was young. I hid parts of myself that I thought he would disapprove and instead, spoke about life in America, our travels abroad, the children, and Norman's retirement. He questioned why, if I was so happy with Norman, would I be socializing at the Golden Fleece with other men? I was in shock and questioned his comment. He said Gloria told him every evening when I left the hospital, I spent my time at the Golden Fleece trying to pick up men. My intuition was correct. The resentment my sister held against me was apparent in her lies.

Gloria reiterated the same story to my mother, telling her I did not care about my father. She said the only reason why I returned to England was to find another husband. This was a lie.

I thought about this situation for years and tried to make sense of it all. I had no idea where she came up with that ridiculous story. I think Gloria was manipulating my parents to make herself look good in their eyes. I loved my sister, but I could not understand why she was so mean during my father's final days. I felt so betrayed. I have eight children at home and I am married. I was not interested in other men.

Before I left England, my mother told me how she wanted to come to America. My mother said she no longer wanted to remain in England once her husband passed away. She did not want to be alone either, and did not want to live in Canada with Gloria and Terry.

I was not by my father's side when he died. I missed his funeral and this deeply hurts me to this day.

Gloria stayed on in England to finalize the estate. I

spoke with her and told her that Mum wanted to move to America. Norman and I would claim her as a dependent and she could receive military benefits. Gloria seemed jealous and insisted Mum move in with her. My mother left England and moved to Canada. Within a few short months afterward, my mother sent a letter asking if she could come to America.

I met her at the airport and noticed she had bruises on her arms. I asked her where the bruises came from and she would not tell me. All she said was that there was no more money in my father's estate. I made her as comfortable as possible. It took some time before she opened up and told me about the hellhole she was living in. She told me that Terry had a fiery temper. It got worse when she told Terry there was no more money in the estate. He then threw a glass ashtray, hitting her in the back of her head, splitting it open. It was only then that she found the strength to leave Canada and come live with us in Kentucky.

After my mother died, Gloria called to tell me that she was seriously ill. We had a very long conversation and we reconciled our differences. We forgave each other. Norman overhead the conversation and could not understand why I forgave her.

"Because she is my sister," I told him.

Indiana University Bloomington
1976

IN BECOMING A nurse, I incorporated a culture of caring by respecting the dignity of each person without conditions or limitations. Nurses hold these values deep inside their being. I began the prerequisite courses at Indiana University Bloomington School of Nursing. This path prepared me for the entry-level professional nursing position, and served as the foundation for my Bachelor of Science in Nursing (BSN) degree.

I studied anatomy, calculus, English, psychology, sociology, and attended the in-person lab classes. One requirement in the laboratory was to wear white nurses' shoes. I did not have the money to buy a pair and instead, I improvised, using regular house paint to dye my brown shoes white. In class, the paint dried, cracked, and flakes fell onto the floor. I realized my dilemma when the instructor approached me, making me aware of my situation. The next day, she handed me a brand new pair of nurses' shoes.

I did not own a watch and I needed one with discernible 5-second increment indicators, which gave an accurate measurement for when I took pulse readings. I used Norman's watch instead. It had a big face and everyone noticed it. They asked me if I needed a nice slim nurses' watch. They told me I could buy a

Timex for next to nothing. What they did not know was that I had nothing, because I was paying for my education. A brand new Timex watch would have been a luxury for me!

I will never forget Norman and all the wonderful things he did for me while I was attending college. In all sorts of weather, he drove two hours each way to and from school. He brought a pillow and slept in the back of the car while I attended classes. When the motor on the windshield wipers broke, I had to reach my arm out of the passenger side, and push the blades back and forth. A driver in the car next to us yelled "Semi-automatic?" and I yelled back, "Yes, of course!" Norman had limited sight and was blind in one eye. He needed my assistance while driving. When the light at the intersection changed, I hollered, "Go! Go!"

At this time, our seventh-born, Marcella, was 13 years old, and she watched over Gunard, and Chris. Terri and Wayne were on their own. Wayne pursued a degree in nursing then left after his first year to work at the USPS because it paid more money. Wayne graduated from Bellarmine University in Louisville. Barry, Gloria, and Joann were practically adults. Even though they were still living at home, they worked full time at their respective jobs.

We lived on Southcrest Drive, and on my days off from school, Gunard, Marcella, Chris and I, would spend the day at Iroquois Park. It is a 739-acre park perched on a large knob, overlooking the city of

Louisville. Covered with old-growth forest, its most prominent feature is the scenic viewpoint atop the hill. Norman would stay home to rest.

I wandered musingly with the kids for hours on the walking trails, listening to the birds chirping, thinking back on my days in Germany. We played in the water park and ate lunch in the picnic area.

The kids nicknamed me 'Mother Nature,' because of the amount of time we spent at the park. While Norman was at home resting, I would take the kids to the park every chance I could get. I enjoyed walking along the mountainous trails, exploring the woods, and sitting in the amphitheater, listening to the musicians play. Sometimes Gunard or Chris would fall down the ditch and I had to pull them out! One time, we parked in the dense forest area and spent hours exploring the woods. When it was time to go home, I noticed we were lost. I had to relieve myself, and when no one was looking, I dropped my pants behind a large tree and went. Thank God, nobody saw me! We walked for hours trying to find the car. At 11 years old, Chris was the sharp one. He noticed that we were walking around in circles, because he yelled out, "Hey Mom! We were here already because that's where you peed!" Eventually, we found the car and piled in. I turned the ignition switch, but the car would not start. I opened the hood and Chris noticed the belt was broken. Thinking quickly, I removed my tights, wove them around the pulleys, and tied them together. Thank God, we were able to get home that day. If it were not for Chris's quick thinking, I would have not known what to do.

In June 1978, I received my Associates Degree in Nursing. My family looked on as I walked across the stage to receive my diploma. I felt so proud. I believe my diploma should have included my daughter, Marcella's name, because she watched over the kids the entire time I was gone.

Jewish Hospital – 1978

I TRANSFERRED TO Spalding University to attain a Bachelor of Science in Nursing (BSN) degree. I found my passion and wanted to become a Certified Nurse in the Operating Room (CNOR). During the day, I attended school, and at night, I worked at the Jewish Hospital, in Louisville, KY, in their operating room as a Scrub Technician/Surgical Technologist.

As I worked under the supervision of a registered nurse, I learned how to prepare the patients for surgery, ensured the operating room was clean and sterile, and assisted the surgeon during the surgical procedures. The work was physically demanding requiring that I stand for long periods in the same location. I worked with the hand specialists, watching how the surgeons reattached hands and scalps. My introduction to the hospital was rather, well, let me tell you how my first day went.

I arrived for my shift, placed my belongings in the locker, and when I returned to my station, a big, black man walked out of the elevator, and pushed me down onto the floor. I thought he was attacking me, but in reality, he was saving my life. Gunshots fired above my head. I thought I was in a war zone. I lay there, pretending I was dead. I was so frightened. The police arrived and hauled two men off to jail. It turns out that a gang member was looking for another gang member. And that my friends, was my first day on the job!

Most patients who arrived in the emergency room were either farmers who had their hands mauled off by a tractor, or women who caught their hair in the motor, ripping off their scalp. We also had corn-picker injuries. These patients had their hands completely de-clubbed. The accident happened when the cob became stuck in the corn sheller. Instead of turning the machine off, they put their hand in to remove the husk.

We received numerous lawnmower injuries. Either the children fell off the riding mower and were ran over, or for some reason, people used their machine as a hedge trimmer. One time, two men used the mower to trim the hedges. Of course, this did not turn out well. The farmer's skin sheared off on his back and buttocks. I came to learn which patients could have their limbs reattached or not.

I scrubbed the hand of Astronaut Neil Armstrong. It was sometime in November 1978. He jumped off the back of his grain truck and his wedding ring became caught in the wheel, tearing off the tip of his ring finger. He collected the severed digit, packed it in ice, and drove himself to the hospital to get it reattached! Can you believe some of the staff members wanted Armstrong's bloody 4 x 4 gauze pads and lap sponges for souvenirs'! I even scrubbed the instruments used on the legendary American singer, Andy Williams.

I received special training in anastomosis. Anastomosis is a surgical connection between two tubular structures, such as blood vessels, or loops of the intestine. For six weeks, I attended classes in the university's morgue to learn how to assist the surgeon in the operating room. I learned various delicate, medical procedures, and dissected rats under the microscope. I learned how to irrigate and apply a continuous solution across an open wound surface to achieve wound hydration, and remove debris. During the visual examination, I watched the surgeon apply sutures thinner than a strand of hair. I trained to use an absorption sponge. This triangular-shaped synthetic surgical sponge is made of soft biocompatible material and absorbs fluids twice as fast as the best cotton sponges, leaving no fiber residue behind.

We had some comical times at the hospital too. One day, I was circulating a craniotomy.[11] I rushed about the OR to the Bovie machine and asked the surgeon what strength he wanted it set at, 35 or 40 amps.[12] Right at that very second, my scrubs dropped down to the floor! I forgot to tie my pants! Here I am standing at the machine, showing my black lace panties, (my daughters of course, not mine), and a nurse from the other room walked in and chuckled.

"Dorothy! You've lost your pants!" She said it so loud that the surgeon, anesthesiologist, and the tech

---

[11] Cleaning the surgical opening of a skull
[12] A pulsing coagulation machine for quick and powerful coagulation of tissue

turned around at the same time and stared at me! What do you think my response was?

"I'll do anything to get attention!" I giggled back.

"Hey Dorothy!" the surgeon shouted. "Make sure your pants are tight and up!" he snickered. Every time thereafter, when I saw him in the hallway, we laughed!

Sometimes, it was so cold in the operating room. I was in the locker room rushing and I forgot to put a shirt on underneath my scrub jacket. I just zipped it up right up over my bra. Now, picture this. Here I am standing in the OR, concentrating on the procedure, and out of nowhere, came one of the hottest hot flashes a woman could get! Naturally, I unzipped and removed my jacket. I was standing in the middle of the OR, unaware that my bra was showing! Everyone started laughing!

"Are we getting a strip-tease here Dot?" the surgeon asked.

"Da, da, da, dah..., da, da, da, dah..." the surgical tech started singing the *Stripper* song by David Rose. Everyone was laughing!

We were such a tight-knit group and everyone loved working together. We were like one great big family!

Another time there was a surgeon who weighed close to four-hundred pounds. He was an ear, nose, and throat doctor. He walked into the OR and lost his pants too! The nurse screamed to me, "Rosie! Pull his pants up!"

I looked at the other nurses and hesitated. I walked up to him and hesitantly said, "Doctor, do you know you lost your pants? I am going to have to pull them up right now."

Oh my God! He was so big around the stomach! He was not wearing his underwear and I accidentally touched his testicles. I was so embarrassed. Sometimes doctors do not wear underwear, because right after surgery, they go directly to the shower and wash.

Now, there I was six months pregnant with our ninth child. It was hard for me to waddle around the operating room. I asked our new scrub technician to get the instruments and place them on the table for me. For some reason, the surgeon became upset with the scrub nurse, and said I had to assist him instead. I was assigned to circulate on this surgery not assist him. I thought to myself, "Noland cannot circulate. The doctor will have to take the heat himself." While I was scrubbing my hand, my pants fell! This time, I was not wearing underwear, only a garter belt and stockings! Noland saw what happened.

"Rosie, I've got to pull your pants up!" Noland said.

"No, don't do that!" I replied. "I'm going to ask to be excused and go out to the sub-sterile room."

The surgeon overheard our conversation and did not allow me to go into the other room. I felt so embarrassed when Noland came over and pulled up and tied my pants. I saw the look on his face and he was embarrassed too!

Another time, I was in such a rush, that I forgot to insert an indwelling catheter into the patient.

"You did put the Foley into him didn't you Rosie?" the surgeon asked.[13]

Oh my God! I remembered that I did not!

On my hands and knees, I crawled underneath the table, felt for the patient's penis, and inserted the plastic tubing. I hit the mark the first time and it slipped it right in!

Another time, I placed an amputated leg in a black, plastic bag on the splash basin, and then completed my task. I needed to take it down to the mortuary. I turned around and it was gone. I immediately informed the surgeon and he told me it was probably down the medical trash chute. I raced downstairs into the basement. Eventually, after going through the trash heap, I found the bag and brought it to the mortuary. The person who the leg belonged to was a Roman Catholic and wanted his leg buried with him.

It is always a difficult time when someone dies under your watch in the OR. This precarious situation involved a horrific automobile accident with a husband and his pregnant wife. Even though she died shortly afterward on the operating table, her unborn child did not. I helped deliver the baby via a C-section. The baby was six weeks premature and died shortly afterward in my arms. The surgical team did everything in their

---

[13] An indwelling catheter with a small balloon filled with a solution that holds the catheter in the bladder

power to save the mother and child. How does one provide insight into describing the dichotomy of balancing death and professional legitimacy? I do not know about anyone else, but I know I felt very depressed. As the surgeon left the room to tell the husband, I cleaned the newborn's lifeless body. I wrapped the baby in cloth, picked her up, and held her close to my chest. As I was carrying her down the hallway to the elevator, a nurse looked at me and snickered, "What's in your arms Rosie?" I could not answer. Tears welled up in my eyes as I pressed the button in the elevator to go down to the morgue. I am not Catholic, but I was that day, and I said a prayer. I gently laid the baby on the table, kissed her forehead, and said "goodbye." It is never easy to develop strong coping skills in the face of death. Each situation is unique unto itself.

"Hey Rosie!" one of the nurses yelled. "You'll never guess what you'll be scrubbing today! Go look on the back table and you'll see two legs sticking up on ice in the bowl," she remarked.

I was horrified. The mangled body of an infant girl lay under anesthesia. One leg gnawed away to the hip. Raw flesh and bones hung from the other stub. Norton's Children's Hospital could not reattach the severed limb. Our specialized team of surgeons worked desperately into the night. It was impossible. The child had died.

The mother was mentally deranged. She became

angry with the infant because she was crying. The mother ended up in Central State Hospital and the father went to prison.

In the seventies, the term 'social injuries of the rectum,' bestowed a certain refined sense of dignity upon an often-solitary ritual. To the embarrassment and personal misery of the patients who embraced this unique lifestyle of insertion, admittance into the operating room meant answering the inevitable question asked by the surgeon; 'Why?' Maybe, the reason could be out of curiosity, since most of the time, it is the man seeking the ultimate erotic stimulation. After all, his rectum, adjacent to the prostate, is the key to male sexuality.

A man came into the emergency room claiming he had a foreign object in his rectum and needed immediate medical attention. I prepared the operating room, scrubbed the patient's buttock area, and the anesthesiologist put him under. Gently, the surgeon probed the area and removed a dead gerbil. I felt so sorry for the gerbil and its horrible demise.

Another time, a male patient inserted a vibrator into his rectum. The muscles contracted and pulled the vibrator into the colon. It had a good set of batteries because it was still vibrating when the surgeon removed it! We found shot glasses, a soda bottle, even a cucumber!

Elements of black humor made light of difficult situations. A 500-pound man straddled on two tables was brought into the operating room. The doctors thought best to give him spinal anesthesia. He was lying on his side and his stomach was hanging out over the table. It was my responsibility to hold him in position as the surgeon gave him the injection. I was barley tall enough to reach my arms over his abdomen to hold him in place. I was so afraid he would roll off the table onto me!

The doctor nudged him forward and I started suffocating! In distress, I waived my arms letting the surgeon know I could not breathe. After the surgery, the doctor apologized. "Boy! That was one hell of a whale! Rosie, I'm so sorry you nearly suffocated."

It was scary working on patients diagnosed with the flesh-eating disease. I had to be very careful when I scrubbed the patient and prepared them for surgery. Necrotizing fasciitis is an infection that results in the death of parts of the body's soft tissue. The disease is severe, comes on suddenly, and spreads rapidly. Symptoms include red or purple skin in the affected area, severe pain, fever, and vomiting. The dead tissue turns black and needs to be surgically removed. I was always careful when working with these patients.

I genuinely loved working at the Jewish Hospital. I did not look at it as having a job. I viewed my position as being part of my lifestyle. I worked upwards of eighteen hours a day. I worked every holiday including Easter, Thanksgiving, Fourth of July, and Christmas. I made a good income and the hospital paid $5 more an hour to hold the beeper. I received time and a half when called in.

The hospital's policy was that everyone had to work their shift, even if they worked a shift the night before. Between my shifts, I rested in the recovery room for an hour, and then worked another shift. I worked my butt off for my family! By this time, Norman was totally disabled, and in failing health.

I was one of the only nurses to train for Intraoperative Blood Salvage (IOS), also known as cell salvage. Today the techs perform this procedure. The IOS is a specific type of autologous blood transfusion, a medical procedure involving recovering blood lost during surgery, and re-infusing it back into the patient. It separates the plasma from the red blood cells. The blood flows from the patient, through a tube, into the centrifuge, and into a bell that I had to seat and twist. You guessed it. Something happened one day.

I was circulating on a thoracotomy using the cell salvage and I did not seat the bell just right.[14] It sounded like a washing machine going off-kilter. I tried seating the bell from rocking and blood was pouring onto the floor.

"I hope that's your damn blood Rosie," the surgeon yelled.

"I have to be excused, doctor. I didn't seat the bell correctly," I embarrassingly replied.

"Turn that damn thing off and hurry it up!" the

---

[14] Surgery to open your chest usually to operate on the lungs.

surgeon screamed!

Oh, the surgeon was so angry with me! Of course, I had to get a new bell, and start the procedure all over from the beginning.

On some days, coming into work was easy, and on other days, it was hard. I never knew what one day to the next would bring. Overall, I enjoyed working at the hospital. The Jewish Hospital was and still is internationally renowned for their advanced technology and innovative leading-edge advancements of being the first in hand transplants. For a year, I did not like working in the ER, however, I loved working in the OR.

On August 21, 1979, in the Sixth Circuit Court in Louisville, Kentucky, I, Dorothy Rose Marie Swanson, was administered my Oath of Citizenship, and was duly sworn into, and became a Naturalized Citizen of the United States of America. My family was so proud of me.

In my final year in college, I received financial assistance from a Jewish women's organization, to pay for my last year in the university. I am sorry I do not remember the name of the organization because it was so long ago. This is when I found out that I could have received 100% financial assistance from the US government because Norman was a disabled veteran.

In June 1980, I passed my Certified Perioperative Nursing (CNOR) test and graduated with a Bachelor of Science in Nursing (BSN) from Spalding University. My mother, Norman, Marcella, and Chris were so proud to see me walk on stage to receive my diploma.

In September 1979, our ninth child, Kathleen, was born.

I admitted Norman into the hospital on January 28, 1981. He was not feeling well. Norman passed away on February 1, 1981, from cardiopulmonary arrest and an old myocardial infarction with ventricular aneurysm. Norman rests at Camp Nelson National Cemetery in Nicholasville, Kentucky. He was the love of my life and he will be my love in death.

My mother stayed with the children and me in Kentucky until she passed away on August 27, 1985. She lies in the Bethany Memorial Cemetery in Valley Station near Lexington, KY.

Humana General Hospital
1985

THE HOUSE FELT so empty with everyone gone except for Marcella, who watched Kathleen while I worked, and Chris, who had a steady full-time job. At this point in my life, I think it was time for a change.

I left the Jewish Hospital and secured a CNOR position in the Trauma Center at Humana General Hospital in Louisville, KY. Surgery works much like a symphony with the conductor being the surgeon, and the perioperative nurses as the orchestra. CNOR's require many years of experience, study, and training to work in the operating room. Surgery requires patience, diligence, and a steady hand, with some operations taking more than 5 hours to complete. This marathon-like focus is what separates OR nurses from Registered Nurses. While they may not be the ones cutting into the patient, their role is equally significant to the success or detriment of the surgery.

Motorcycle accident victims were the worst that came into the ER. The tech and I assessed the patient to see whether they are a candidate for the OR. If they were, we would call the OR asking them to prepare the room. More than ninety percent of the hospital patients were indigents and unable to pay their bills.

Three adolescent boys involved in an automobile

accident came into the OR. My responsibility was to prepare them for surgery. I walked into the room, looked down, and saw my son Chris! I ran out of the room screaming, "That's my son! That is my son! I can't scrub this case!"

"It's got to be someone that looks like your son," a nurse said, trying to reassure me.

To be on the safe side, the nurse suggested I call home and confirm that it is not Chris. These boys arrived from Indiana and we live in Kentucky. Marcella told me Chris went over to his friend's house in Indiana. I dropped the phone and insisted that the boy in the OR was my son. Regardless, I had to perform my duty. Assigned to another boy, I scrubbed the blood from his body, and prepared him for surgery, all the while thinking about my son in the OR room. A million questions raced through my mind. It was difficult to focus on the boy in my care. I had to put Chris out of my mind and concentrate, because this patient's life depended upon my competence. After surgery, I was relieved to find out that the lad in the other operating room was not my son. By God! This boy was Chris's doppelganger!

Ensuring a patient's safety in the operating room begins even before the patient enters the operative suite, and includes attention to all applicable types of preventable medical errors. On this particular procedure, I assisted a surgeon on a laparotomy.[15] I

---

[15] A surgical incision into the abdominal cavity

admit I am not perfect. However, some people can be outright idiots! A surgeon started the Bovie machine without a perioperative nurse present when the patient's colon was out of the stomach. Usually, the colon is placed in a bag with moist towels, and usually, the surgeon feels along the colon for blockage. If the surgeon finds a blockage, the contents are removed by either performing a colonoscopy or a surgical anastomosis.[16]

"Hey Rosie! What are you having for supper tonight?" the surgeon jokingly questioned.

"You've got stew there! All you have to do is add carrots and peas!" I answered.

I did not know what this surgeon thought he was doing. He was coagulating something that was bleeding and BAM! The colon exploded all over the OR. The anesthesiologist jumped off his stool and ran behind his machine. I could not run fast enough. Thank God, I was wearing my face shield and scrubs. The patient's feces splashed all over the room, including myself, and the surgeon. The doctor left the room to wash up while I continued circulating the patient.

Every once in a while, there comes a time in our life when we may be released from our job. Losing a job is very stressful and can cause feelings of grief and resentment. My thinking is this; you can sulk in either self-pity and depression or, build-up your self-

---

[16] A surgical technique used to make a new connection between two body structures that carry fluid, such as blood vessels or bowel.

confidence to make a new way in life. Human Resources released me from my CNOR position because there was an abundance of nurses and I had less seniority. I believed in myself, in my skills, and my education. This was a pivotal moment in my life. I could stay in Kentucky or I can make a life style change. The director told me there were openings at the Humana Hospital Sunbay in St. Petersburg, Fl. I went home that evening to discuss the opportunity with my daughter and grandson. We decided to move to the Sunshine State.

Relocating to Florida – 1986

I MOVED TO Florida in 1986 with Kathleen and my grandson. My other children remained in Kentucky, because they were married and had children, except for Gunard. He was in the military. Eventually, my children moved to Florida.

After we settled into the new apartment, I made an appointment to meet with the Director of Human Resources at Humana Hospital Sunbay. The director met with me and said they did not have any openings at their facility. I was disappointed. I thought, "Maybe God has other plans for me." I set off to look for employment elsewhere.

I secured a position at St. Anthony's Hospital in St. Petersburg. Eventually, the hospital became BayCare. With 7 years' experience in the operating room, holding an RN license, with a Bachelor of Science in Nursing, and Certified Perioperative Nurse credentials, my starting wage was $9.00 an hour.

The Franciscan Sisters of Allegany founded St. Anthony's Hospital with a mission to serve. They refused abortions even if the mother's life depended upon it. I signed a statement promising that I would not participate in an abortion. I had to keep to my word.

I did the best I could. However, some difficult situations call for being out of integrity, and I assisted a surgeon in an abortion. The mother had a severe heart condition and could not keep this baby. She became pregnant even though the doctors advised against it. The surgeon inserted a tube through the cervix and into the uterus. The machine gently sucked out the pregnancy tissue into the machine. For years afterward, I had horrible nightmares of the baby screaming inside the mother's uterus as its body ripped apart.

The nuns were very kind and considerate with the patients, talking with them before they went into surgery, and praying for them, and their well-being during, and after surgery. Everyone was kind and compassionate.

I had the opportunity to work with a black surgeon who asked me if I minded working with him.

"You are a surgeon and I am a Scrub and Circulating Nurse. Why would I mind working with you?" I said.

"There are some people who do not want to work with me because I am black," he replied.

A patient assigned to us assumed she was pregnant. The doctor performed an exploratory Laparotomy and found a large cyst weighing in at 15 pounds.[17] Hair and teeth filled the cyst. It was probably a fetus at one time. Unfortunately, the doctor had to perform a

---

[17] A surgical incision into the abdominal cavity, for diagnosis or in preparation for surgery.

hysterectomy that denied her, her future motherhood.

AIDS was ravaging the world at this time. Many were unsure of the cause of HIV. I noticed many patients who came into the OR carried the symptoms. I used to wash the instrumentation without wearing medical latex gloves. I was well aware of the risks I was taking. However, I could not work well wearing those gloves.

On a different note, please do not get me wrong when I say I heard too many nurses complain about having to work beyond their normal shifts. I took every call that came in. Sometimes, I worked seven days a week. I filled in for the nurses on the night shift, and worked until six in the morning. Then, I had to pull my regular day shift, which started at seven o'clock. If I was lucky, I might get an hour's sleep in the recovery room. Not once did I complain to management. Not once did I say "No." I believed it was my duty to be in the OR when I was called upon. Maybe, my thinking is different. After Norman became disabled, I was the head of the household. I worked to support a family of eleven. What else was I going to do? My family came first and I did everything in my power to make sure the kids had a roof over their heads, food in their bellies, and warm beds to sleep in at night.

Northside Hospital – 1987

FROM ST. ANTHONY'S Hospital, I secured a position as the Director of Operations at the Metropolitan Hospital in Pinellas Park. FL. I oversaw ICU, GI, EGD's, and Outpatient Surgery.[18] I was in a salaried position and did not receive overtime for the additional hours I worked. Every day, I addressed a tremendous amount of paperwork. I could not type, and therefore, I hired and paid a typist, out of my pocket $1.50 a page, to do my reports. After working there for five years, I said this is stupid and enough is enough. I handed in my resignation and left.

I started work as a CNOR at Northside Hospital in St. Petersburg, FL. The hospital provided a variety of amenities including comprehensive emergency, diagnostic, medical-surgical, and women's services including labor and delivery, post-partum, and nursery services.

Most of the employees particularly hated one surgeon. He was a very small Asian man, with a tremendous ego, and he would constantly yell at everyone. During a hysterectomy, the surgeon became angry, and after removing the uterus, he threw it at me! It missed me by inches. Throwing uteruses, instruments or knives in the operating room during the

---

[18] ICU–Intensive Care Unit, GI-Gastrointestinal, EGD–Esophagogastroduodenoscopy

AIDS epidemic was unprofessional on his part. Employees were afraid of him and now I knew why.

The next time I worked with him, I made sure the instruments were in a kidney basin on the table. I did not want anyone to get hurt.

"Have you started putting the leads on before the anesthesiologist gets here?" he yelled, directing his attack on me.

"Yes sir they are in place," I replied. Then he said something that 'got my goat.' I cannot remember exactly what he said but what he said made my blood boil. In the OR, stools are available for the shorter doctors so that they can stand on them to operate. I could not help myself. Something snapped inside my head. I placed my foot on that stool, mustered up my courage, and shoved the stool straight towards him.

"Here's your manhood, D-O-C-T-O-R!" I sarcastically replied.

He reported me to the office. Human Resources called me into the office and I had to apologize to him.

After that incident, the atmosphere calmed down in the OR. I surprised myself when I spoke with him about a black mole on my child's back. He said he would look at it. The doctor recommended removing the mole because it was melanoma.

"Not to worry Rosie. I'll do deep margins and I'm sure I'll be able to get it all out," the surgeon said in a reassuring tone.

The tissue went to the lab for analysis and all I could do was wait for the results. I found myself in the OR getting ready for the next operation when the doctor walked in. He did not say anything. I thought the test result would have returned by now. Very calmly, and with great compassion, the surgeon looked up from the procedure and said, "Rosie, I need to talk to you. Please come into the doctors' lounge after we are finished here."

I completed my duties and hurriedly rushed into the doctor's lounge.

"Rosie, please sit down. It is exactly what I thought it was. It is a bad case of melanoma. Do not worry about the surgery. I am going to handle it and you will not have to pay for anything. Not even the hospital bill. I will pay for everything," he said.

I began crying with both tears of anguish and tears of joy. "Oh my God! You are going to do that for me after the way I treated you?" I cried. I felt so guilty.

"Dorothy," he said, addressing me by my formal name. "I see you are an excellent scrub nurse. You treat everyone fairly with compassion. I see the long hours you put into your job. If anyone deserves a break, it is you. Do not worry about a thing. Everything is prepared. Now go home and be with your family. I will see you soon."

I could have given him the biggest hug, but I dared not. Other doctors were in the room and I did not want anyone spreading rumors. I thanked him and God with all my heart. Even though he continued to yell at everyone else, I treated him with respect. Although the surgeon and I found respect for one another, my co-workers and I did not.

The silent killer of workplace happiness, productivity and health, is a lack of basic civility, namely workplace bullying. I found myself amongst persistent verbal and nonverbal aggression at work, including personal attacks, and a multitude of other painful and sometimes hostile interactions. The nurses made it difficult for me to perform my job. They hid my equipment, removed my paperwork from the patient's notebook, and threw it away. They verbally abused me, telling me to, "Go back to England!" because I took a job away from an American nurse. I learned through the grapevine the reason they were bullying me was that I did not conceal the affair between a nurse and a surgeon. I live my life with integrity and high morals, values, ethics, principles, and standards. That is what the nurses had against me. I would not comply with their clique.

In turn, the accused surgeon denied me access to work in the OR. I was on call and no one else was available to assist him on a ruptured brain aneurysm. The surgeon told me to find someone else.

After the surgery, the doctor complimented and thanked everyone in the OR but not me.

For Christmas, this same specialist gave everyone in the OR a box of pecans.

For seven years, my performance never swayed or faltered. I was steadfast and focused. I was there to do a job not to placate to their unruly and disruptive behaviors. Finally, I had enough. I said, "I am done! I am finished!" I left Northside without even giving notice. With my head held high, I walked out the front door.

Hospice Villas – 1990

MY DUTIES AS a Charge Nurse at the Pinellas Park, Florida, Hospice Villas-Woodside included overseeing operations, monitoring admissions and discharges, and directing and overseeing the activities of the nursing and support staff. I planned and maintained the schedule of the staff and worked on the unit's budget. My responsibilities also included monitoring inventories of supplies and medicines, and working closely with the unit manager.

Led by the staff of volunteers from the Bereavement Team, the memorial ceremonies held in our chapel provided a time for reverence, prayer, and reflection, for those residents who had passed. Friends of the deceased, along with their family, and staff, were welcomed to attend. I attended a service with a technician co-worker from India, named Kolli. We were the only staff members attending. After the service, I called out to him.

"Hey! Where are you going Kolli?" I asked.

"Mrs. Swanson. I must go back to floor," he said in his Hindi dialect.

"Oh no, you don't! You have to stay right here because, with your accent and skin color, someone will think you are a terrorist!" I jokingly said to him.

The next day, the Human Resource Director called me into his office. I had to apologize to Kolli.

"I am so sorry for what I said to you yesterday, Kolli. I was only joking around. I will never do it again, I promise," I said with sincerity in my heart.

He hugged me. "I know you were joking around. These people are crazy for asking you to apologize to me. It's alright," he compassionately replied.

We understood each other because we were friends. Every day, Kolli would bring lunch to my desk. I would ask him to get me something specific and he always returned with something different.

"Hey Kolli! I didn't ask for that!" I said in a playful tone.

"I know. You need to eat healthy food," he would tell me.

I never received the lunch I ordered. Kolli enjoyed his job as much as I did. He worked as many hours as I, was compassionate towards the residents and family members, and worked well with the employees. I truly loved him as a person. He was a good man.

Donated flowers from 'Random Acts of Flowers,' were a way to brighten our facility. In the maintenance room, Kolli and I separated the variety of flowers from the complimentary greenery, snipped the bottoms of the stems, and rearranged the pieces into new bouquets. Placed in vases, we distributed our collection throughout the building, and around my workstation. Co-workers admired my flowers, but not the Executive Director.

"Dorothy Swanson!" I heard my name called.

"These flowers have to go right now! I can't see you and neither can the families," the Executive Director said peering over my flower wall.

"Well that's I point," I smartly answered back.

"Don't be a smarty-pants! I do not want any more discussion. This is not Garden Avenue! This is Hospice! Get rid of those flowers at once!" she retorted.

Reluctantly, I removed the potted plants from my desk and placed them in the resident's rooms.

My promotion as the Evening Nurse Supervisor came after my annual performance review. I made decisions Johnny-on-the-spot. At other times, confrontations with personnel were like talking to a brick wall. At precisely 8:00 p.m., I locked the front door. The safety of my residents was my top priority and I held steadfast. Anyone wishing to enter past that hour could simply ring the bell for admittance.

"You can't lock the front door! Some people come in at night to visit their relatives!" the Executive Director shouted.

I calmly responded, validating her concern and informed her that the door will remain locked.

"No one is going to come in here and hurt anyone," she replied.

"Oh?" I said questioning her authority.

"No! Not no one!" she snorted, turned and walked away.

I did not listen to her. I listened to my intuition instead. It was a good call on my part because one evening a man came up to the door and started banging on it.

"What do you need?" I asked.

"I need to use your telephone right now! I have an emergency," this man said.

"Don't you have a cell phone?" I questioned.

"No! I can't afford one," he replied.

"Tell me what your emergency is and I will call someone for you," I responded.

"Never mind," he said and stormed away.

From that moment on, I kept the front doors locked. I did not care if the Executive Director fired me or not!

In 2000, Hospice Villas received a comatose patient named Terri. Her husband Michael was a very caring man. He told me he tried everything to stimulate the brain, from electrical stimulation treatments to hiring a private nurse. Nothing worked.

Teri was in an irreversible persistent vegetative state. For most of the day, Terri continuously sat in a medical recliner, looking out her bedroom window, or passively engaging in Life Enrichment activities. She received nutrition from the feeding G-tube in her abdomen. Her husband Michael spent hours visiting her, and on many occasions, her family would visit.

Before she retired for the evening, I made sure her legs were elevated. This therapy relieved the pressure in the arteries and encouraged blood flow out from the legs to course through the rest of her body. Terri never startled the time I replaced the feeding bag and dropped it onto the floor. The only time she showed a reaction was when she was on her menstrual cycle. She moaned and tears ran down her face. To help with her discomfort, the nurses administered morphine drops under her tongue.

I remember the first time her parents and sister arrived at the facility. They appeared disheveled. The family walked into Terri's room and I saw the father pull the television around so that he could watch his sports. I specifically left it on the animal channel. I do not remember the father showering love or affection over his daughter. On the other hand, her mother was very attentive and showered her daughter in love. The sister well, from what I saw, not so much. On every visit, unfortunately, the father seemed to find problems with his daughter's care. A team of health care professionals meticulously cared for Terri. We did everything possible to make Terri comfortable. One time, she did have a tooth pulled, but that was about it.

Someone reported the facility to the State of Florida. Behind closed doors, the state inspected her body for abrasions. They inspected the cleanliness of her room, the G-tube, her laundry, personal items, and bedding. They spoke with the Executive Director, nurses, CNA's, and reviewed her Care Plan and paperwork. The State always found our commitment, dedication, and service to our residents, on the highest of standards.

Hospice had purchased a special $10,000.00 bed for Terri that would automatically turn her from side to side. Terri received personalized care. Her husband, Michael, requested every morning that Terri's make-up be applied and that she is placed in the chair by the window every morning.

When Terri's parents came in with a police officer, I noticed how their entire appearance had changed. Now, they were dressed impeccably. When they left the building, I noticed they were driving a brand new car. I heard they had flown to Rome to see the Pope. The media attention was giving the family all this fame. I heard the family set up a foundation for their daughter and people started giving them money.

The public never saw the love Michael showed for his wife or his face when he left the room. Michael was motivated in pursuing the best medical care for Terri. He would come in unexpectedly to make sure we were fulfilling his wishes. By this time, I knew Michael for three years.

"Thank you Dorothy for taking such good care of my wife," Michael would say on so many occasions. He always addressed me by my formal name.

"Michael, I care for you and your wife. I am so sorry that she is in this condition. I feel terrible about the coverage you are receiving from the media because you do not deserve that."

I am not sure, but I believe he had to move, because people found out where he was living. I heard they started camping out on his front lawn, harassing him. Those people had no idea what Michael was going through!

One day, the Police arrived to guard Terri's room twenty-four hours a day. On the news, I heard Michael met with the judge and asked for the removal of his wife's feeding tube. The judge approved his request.

Michael came in practically every day to sit with his wife. Occasionally, he brought his girlfriend. The girlfriend sat in the waiting area. I always saw him coming out of the room crying.

"Dorothy, I've waited for her to hold my hand but there is nothing there," he said.

"We are all praying for your wife," I responded. I felt sorry for Michael and the entire family. This case was becoming world news and no one had a moment of peace.

When I was not busy, I visited with Terri and her family. We spoke about her prognosis, her care, and their hopes. When the room fell silent, the mother asked me to get her a bottle of water. I returned and handed her the bottle. I thought it was strange when she repeated her request. I left the room to fulfill her wishes.

When I returned, the parents stood up, and told me they were leaving. I noticed Terri's back was towards the window and I turned her around. It was not until that evening when we used the Hoyer lift to pick her up and place her into the bed. I pulled back on the blanket, and noticed a small funnel on her lap. I thought, "Now, that's funny. Where did this come from?" When I examined her more closely, I noticed that her feeding tube was on the backside of her chair. When I first left the room, the feeding tube was on her left side. I thought to myself, "What happened here?

When I put Terri to bed, I noticed needle marks on her leg. Without hesitation, I called Michael, and told him what I saw. He told me to call her doctor immediately, and to have her taken to the emergency room at Dunedin Hospital. He wanted a full examination of his wife performed. I followed his instructions, but to me, it sounded peculiar. Terri returned to Hospice the following day. When I confronted the parent's about the funnel and needle marks, they denied the accusation. The next day, I received a summons to appear in court. I was one of the eighteen witnesses to testify.

Nervously, I entered the Pinellas County courtroom with a couple of nurse's aides who accompanied me for support. The courtroom was packed. Terri's husband and family were there along with their attorneys. Paperwork piled high on the tables and a large board showed CAT scans of her brain. Every single television crew from FOX, ABC, NBC, and CBS were there.

"Dorothy Swanson?" I heard my name called. I took the stand.

The trial was to determine Terri's wishes and was under the direction of Judge George Greer. Depositions from Michael, Michael's brother, and sister-in-law, recounted statements made proximate to the family, about Terri's wishes. She did not want to remain on artificial life support should she become incapacitated.

On the other hand, Terri's parents indicated that if Terri had provided clear directives, she would have wanted artificial life support.[19] With my hand on the Bible, I swore in.

"Do you promise to tell the truth, the whole truth, and nothing but the truth, so help you God?" was asked of me.

"I do," I nervously replied.

"Please be seated."

The attorney asked for my name, address, where I worked, my position, in what capacity had I known the Petitioners, Respondents, and the Ward, Terri.

Attorney: "Do you think Terri's mother or father would hurt her?"

Swanson: "No. Why would they?"

Attorney: "Don't they visit regularly?"

Swanson: "Yes. The times they would visit, the door was usually closed. When I entered the room, I noticed the channel had been turned to the sports station when I left it on the animal channel. I was hoping the program would get her attention."

---

[19] Florida governor's office executive order number 03-201 – https://www.mayoclinicproceedings.org/article/S0025-6196(11)61439-0/fulltext - Reference # 10 – The Terri Schiavo Saga: The Making of a Tragedy and Lessons Learned, C. Christopher Hook, M.D., Paul S. Mueller, M.D.

Attorney: "Can you tell us how to irrigate a feeding tube, and how you put the food in the tube."

Swanson: The surgeon uses an endoscope to place the G-tube directly into the stomach. The surgeon creates a stoma, a visible opening that connects to the feeding tube outside the body. The feeding tube allows people to take specialized liquid nutrition directly into the stomach. The feeding bottle hangs on the pole, and I check to make sure all the air is out, and to make sure there was no gas inside the tube."

Attorney: "Before your shift, did you get a report from another nurse informing you of her condition?" The attorney handed me a piece of paper.

Swanson: "No. They did not give me any time. I received a tape recording of the report."

Attorney: "What did the tape recording say?"

Swanson: "It said the name of the patient, their room number, and exactly what was done for them, how they looked, how they behaved, any abnormalities, remarks, or issues. It was a complete report.

Attorney: "Do you have any ill feelings against the family?"

Swanson: "Absolutely not! Why would I?"

Attorney: "We have been told that you are not a very compassionate nurse especially when talking to the family."

Swanson: "I think I talk to them exactly how I talk to any of the patient's family and how I am speaking to you right now. I've never been accused of speaking unkindly to any family member, ever."

Judge Greer gave the orders to have the feeding tube removed.

"It's defeating the purpose, Dorothy," Michael said compassionately on one of his regular visits. I tried to explain to him that she would feel no pain.

Crowds of people from all over the country were outside the facility with signs saying 'Let Terri Live,' 'Thou Shall Not Kill!' and 'Starvation is Murder!' Someone had a poster board of the Ten Commandments, while others had red tape stuck over their mouths with the word 'Life.' Someone else held up a sign that read 'Auschwitz USA." Children were running up to the front door with bottles of water. Police officers were trying to keep the people at bay.

Governor Bush sent in the State Troopers to remove Terri from our facility. The doctor received orders to re-insert the feeding tube. The Clearwater Police came on the scene telling the State Troopers to leave. Sharpshooters were on the roof of Hospice. Police dogs guarded the grounds. The school shut down across the street. People said doctors were outside with diagrams of her brain shouting, "There is activity!"

Michael had two neurosurgeons thoroughly check her brain activity. Terri was brain dead.

I watched a segment on the news that showed Terri and her mother. The news made it look like Terri was following a balloon with her eyes, blinking, and moaning. In another scene, her mother held up blinking lights.

When I was alone with Terri in her room, I would stroke her eyelids, and she never blinked. I talked to her compassionately and told her that we were doing everything possible to help her. Every day, I prayed to God, asking him to intervene in her suffering.

One day, I arrived at Hospice and noticed some nurses did not want to go inside the building because they were afraid of all of the people outside. Just as I was opening the door to walk inside the facility, a man ran across the street towards me and screamed, "You're a murderer! You're a murderer!"

When I left work that evening, another man ran up to my vehicle, pulled outward on my driver's side window, and broke the glass. Then, he proceeded to pull off my mirror. He was belligerent, screaming at the top of his lungs, calling me a bitch, and how could I live with myself.

The next day, I told Hospice that I could no longer care for Terri because I felt it was becoming too dangerous. Hospice was relying on me, but I told them I could not take the stress any longer. Hospice moved Terri to the other side of the building. I was relieved that I did not have to take care of her anymore, and at the same time, I felt sad. Terri's room was now empty.

On March 18, 2005, the doctor removed Terri's feeding tube, and on March 31, she expired. There was a big hole in my heart. I cared for Terri. I spent all my holidays with her. I felt deep down inside that she was finally at peace.

When a resident died, the room was thoroughly cleaned, and kept vacant for twenty-four hours. I lit an electric candle in her honor and placed a red rose on her bed. My prayers and thoughts went out to her and her husband.

After her autopsy, Michael had Terri cremated. Her ashes lie interred at Sylvan Abbey Memorial Park in Clearwater, Florida. The epitaph placed by her husband reads:

"I kept my promise."

Occasionally, when a person died, I noticed some had such agonizing expressions on their face. When Terri died, she looked very peaceful, and at rest. I knew in my heart that she went to a good place. I cannot explain it any other way. Another time, a nurse called me into a resident's room, because she saw an angel. I did not see an angel standing by the bed as the nurse had suggested. What I did see however, was the radiant glow on the man's face. He appeared at peace.

This is why I am not afraid of dying. I have seen too many people die in my lifetime. I believe there are only two places one can go for eternity after we expire. It all depends upon how we treat one another while we are alive.

The Human Spirit

HOSPICE RECOGNIZES MANY faiths. Hospice specialists know that when facing a terminal illness at the end of life, many people find themselves reflecting on existential questions. *Who am I? How have I lived my life? Did I make a difference in the lives of others?* Please do not wait until the end of your life to ask these questions. Ask these questions now while you are still alive.

A family member of a Mormon resident told me that they believed the soul separates from the body immediately following death. Their belief is that the soul is judged once a person passes and will be judged one more time when the Resurrection occurs. A map with numerous pushpins hung on the wall. When I asked the family about it, they told me which family their beloved one wanted to be born into. They believe in reincarnation. When the woman died, the minister asked me to hold her in my arms and tell her that she is now safe. I did as they asked.

A resident of the Wicca faith passed. The family wore black robes and carried into the room what appeared to be a dead bird in a cage. A candle burnt on the nightstand. Everyone knelt around the bed and prayed.

"I'm sorry, but you can't have that candle burning. It is against fire regulations. Open flames cannot be in the room. I have an electric candle you can use," I said compassionately.

They respected my request and put out the candle. I never did find out what they did with the caged bird. I could not run out of the room fast enough. They believe in witches and all kinds of goddesses.

A Muslim resident did not have long to live. The entire family was present, sitting around the bed, praying. They invited me to sit in with them. I did not understand what they were saying though I respected their custom. I joined in when everyone shouted "Hallelujah!" With hands held out, palms open, they asked Allah to intercede. They were very nice people.

Another time, a family of a Christian Scientologists resident would not allow the doctors to look at him. They only had their leaders present.

The human spirit, like the mind and body, is a natural dimension of every one of us. It is our awareness of our place in the world, our relations with others, and our overall sense of meaning and purpose in life.

On Christmas, I placed a manger scene in my office. The Executive Director told me to remove it, even though a menorah was present in a Jewish family's room. Hospice is non-denominational.

A nurse showed me a sore she had on her tongue. I told her to have it examined immediately. She thought it was a cold sore. I suspected it might be cancer. I am not a doctor and I cannot give a medical diagnosis under my license. It turned out the nurse had cancer. She never missed a day at work. She was young, had a positive outlook on life, and when she came to work, her focus was on the residents, not on her problems. The doctors placed a feeding tube inside her stomach because she lacked the strength to eat enough to stay healthy. I watched as she fed herself with a syringe. Hospice said she could take off as much time as she wanted but she never did. I think this was the first time I thought about mortality and how short life is. Not long afterward she died. God has taken another beautiful soul from us to sit by his side.

Billy was one of our youngest residents. Diagnosed with AIDS, he did not hide the fact that he was homosexual. He became infected when he slept with someone he did not know on a cruise. He was twenty-seven years old and such a bright, upbeat, young man. We had so many conversations and I enjoyed playing cards with him. I changed his dressing without wearing gloves. I could not wear those rubber gloves! They restricted the functioning of my hands to perform. Billy was so thoughtful.

"Rosie, please put your gloves on. I don't want you to catch what I have," he compassionately said.

"I'm going to die of something one day Billy but today is not that day," I replied.

Billy told me that he forgave the person who gave him AIDS. He said "It's not how many people will remember me when I'm gone. It's about how many people's lives I touch while I am alive."

His mother was jealous of me. I noticed the way she looked at me. For some reason, she always interrupted our conversation. I think it was because she thought we were getting a little too close. Shortly thereafter, Billy's mother transferred him to another unit. After he died, she gave everyone on the floor a gift from him. I did not receive a gift.

I place more value in relationships with those I love than in materialistic things. What one says and does, means more to me than anything else in the world. A person's behavior tells me whether they are living their life with integrity.

At the memorial service, Billy's mother sat in the front row. It was a beautiful service and I thought back upon my short time with him. I walked up to his mother, looked her straight in the eyes, and said, "You know, Billy touched me in many ways. He taught me more in the short time we had together than I could have ever learned from anyone else. He taught me how to love and how to forgive."

Do you know what Billy's mother did next? In front of everyone in the Hospice chapel, she shoved me!

"Here! Billy left this for you!" she sarcastically remarked, pushing the gift into my chest practically knocking me backward. She walked away. I opened the card. It read:

"Thank you Dorothy for everything you have done for me. I love you and I will always be there watching over you."

Love, Billy

Tears came to my eyes.

Billy's mother could have torn up the card and thrown away the present. I was so happy she decided to give it to me. I was not expecting anything. I opened the box and inside was a beautiful pearl crucifix. For years, it hung in my living room. Now it is gone. I asked everyone in my family about the whereabouts of my crucifix. Nobody knows where it is. I wish I had my pearl crucifix. It means so much to me.

Sometimes, AIDS patients can take care of themselves. We had a female resident with AIDS and she was unable to pay towards her residency. I prepared a plate of leftover food from the kitchen and gave it to her. The Unit Manager discovered my intention and reprimanded me for my efforts.

In 2008, at the age of seventy-two, I retired from Hospice. I returned to England one last time and said goodbye to my country. I left my past behind. Now, my memories are preserved for my family and generations to come.

Words of Thought

BEFORE I EXPIRE, I would first like to tell my children, how very proud I am of each of you, and all of what you have accomplished. I love you equally with all my heart. I hope you have taken away a little bit of my principles, and if not, re-read this book again!

Principles are what you stand by in life and values are what you stand around in amongst your family and friends. Principles are stern and unyielding while values are warm and supportive.

A person who knows the difference between right and wrong and chooses right is moral. A person whose morality reflects in his willingness to do the right thing – even if it is hard or dangerous – is ethical. Ethics are moral values in action.

Do you live your life with integrity? I hope I did. Integrity is the practice of being honest and showing a consistent and uncompromising adherence to strong morals. When I meet my maker, I will stand before him and say, "I did my best. No regrets."

Not everything in my life went on as planned. Life does not work that way. Life brings forth situations and it is up to each one of us to learn and make it the best we can – for everyone involved. Our actions or lack thereof, has a rippling effect on those around us, even strangers. Decisions made years ago are in direct correlation to where we are today. It is not up to someone else to make you happy. It is up to you to make yourself happy.

Do you know who you are? Have you ever taken the time to find out what makes you tick? We are in a state of being and need to feel important to have a sense of purpose in life. It is said, "Thoughts become words, words become actions, actions become character, and character is everything." Who you are and who you become are a part of your personality that develops through learning and experience. This is your character. Your behavior, your cognition, and your emotional patterns, having evolved from biological and environmental factors, becomes your personality.

I hope you understand that I did my best in raising you. During the difficult times, I had to go outside my boundaries to protect you. It is a mothers' instinct to sacrifice her well-being when protecting her children. Your welfare superseded my happiness. I always thought about you first.

I am in the twilight of my years. Trust me when I say, "Life goes by in the blink of an eye." Make the most of it. My mind is strong and I am aware. I cannot say much for my body though, it still moves along. "It is not the years honey; it's the mileage," my favorite quote from *Indiana Jones's Raiders of the Lost Ark* movie. Once, I was a vibrant and young girl, full of enthusiasm for life. Now I am old.

We find ourselves in unusual circumstances today. The year the world stood still – 2020. As I find myself at this stage in my life, 84 years old and recuperating in the hospital, having been a nurse, I have been trying to make sense of everything going on with the Novel Coronavirus.

Because of this situation, no one can visit me. As so many are in hospitals and nursing homes, I can only imagine the detachment, they are feeling now, the grief, the sorrow, and the loneliness.

Tomorrow, I will be home, but today is the world we live in. The message I leave with you is this:

Be a reflection of what you would like to see in others. If you want love, give love. If you want honesty, give honesty. If you want respect, give respect. You get in return what you give.

Do not take anything for granted. Focus on life and living. Focus on love. Focus on your children. How can you make a better world for them to live in?

Do not give into materialistic things that need endless maintenance. Instead, focus on spending time with your family. Make memories. Talk. Hug. Hold someone's hand and tell them how much you love them. Listen when they speak. Do not interrupt, for what they say is important, to them. When you respond, do not attack. Validate their words. Show empathy for those less fortunate. Put yourself in their shoes. Help as much as you can but do not let others take advantage of you. Do not take advantage of another's kindness either. Open your heart to understanding.

Learn as much as you can. Remember, you can do anything you put your mind to doing.

Show kind gestures. Write a note, leave a card, or bring flowers. Allow your partner to sleep in, prepare their favorite meal, and offer a kind word of affection. Hug more often. Goodwill is free.

Marriage is not hard work. The first step is to stop expecting a relationship to be perfect or easy. Do not jump to the conclusion that it is the wrong relationship when there are struggles. A good partner gives you emotional support and companionship. Do not give away your powers. Learn to stand on your own two feet and stop compromising. Collaborate instead. A marriage can build us up or it can rip us apart. It is an inter-dependent relationship on each other. Interdependence involves a balance of self and others within the relationship, recognizing that both partners are working to be present and meet each other's physical and emotional needs in appropriate and meaningful ways.

Dream and dream big. Live your life with enthusiasm. Wake up each morning knowing that a new day awaits you. How you think when you awake is how your day will go. Think positive thoughts and you will have a positive day.

Safeguard your wellbeing. Set boundaries. Boundaries are flexible. Walls are not.

We carry loads of internal baggage, battle scars from past hurts, and our defenses become walls built for protection. Those barriers are obstacles on the road to getting close to someone. Drop the walls. Become vulnerable. Stop being defensive and instead, embrace life.

Learn to be open to new experiences. Be open to communicating. Be honest. Be calm. Be optimistic.

Life is not hard. It is only our perception that makes us think it is hard. Be open and receptive to all good things. Stop worrying, especially about what other people think about you. Only you know the truth.

Make a plan and take action. Only those who take action towards their dreams fulfill their goals in life. Be persistent. Dreams do come true.

Laugh with me. Laugh about life's experiences. We learn through our experiences and trust me; I have had 84 years' worth of them. And with this, my dear family and friends, everything must end. With the last page turned in my memoir, know that you are the best chapters in my life. Do not cry for me when I am gone. Rejoice in knowing that I lived a fulfilling life. Rejoice with me instead.

Love,
Mum

Goodnight Children Everywhere

Sleepy little eyes in a sleepy little head,
Sleepy time is drawing near.
In a little while you'll be tucked up in your bed,
Here's a song for baby dear.

Goodnight children everywhere,
Your mummy thinks of you tonight.
Lay your head upon your pillow,
Don't be a kid or a weeping willow.

Close your eyes and say a prayer,
And surely you can find a kiss to spare.
Though you are far away, she's with you night and day,
Goodnight children everywhere

Soon the moon will rise, and caress you with its beams,
While the shadows softly creep.
With a happy smile you will be wrapped up in your
dreams,
Baby will be fast asleep.

Goodnight children everywhere.

History of Collier's End

Situated just to the south of the Roman crossroads is Colliers End, where the minor road from Verulamium crossed Ermine Street on the way to Camulodunum (Colchester). There may have been a few small buildings here and a wooden bridge over the stream just to the south of the village, near Labdens. This name is derived from the 14th century name Lapdenbrigge, meaning the bridge in the valley. A causeway was built at the beginning of the 19th century and the stream was run through a tunnel.

Nicholas le Colyere gave his name to the village, according to the Assize Rolls of 1278 and by 1526, the place was called Colyersend, with end meaning a hamlet. The inhabitants earned their livelihoods from agriculture with its associated crafts and from the important road traffic on what was the old North Road. At Wadesmill, the country's first turnpike was built and the road from London to Cambridge was the first to have milestones.

In 1784, it was in Colliers End that the first ever balloon flight over England came to rest. The pilot, Vincenzo Lunardi, already paused his journey in Welham Green to let his sick cat get off!

At Colliers End, there was a weighbridge. According to the 1840 tithe map, it shows the Weighbridge House on the site of the old army camp.

Not only corn but also coal was carried through the village by horse-drawn wagons between the canals leading to Cambridge and the river Lee from Ware to London. The coaches passed through Colliers End, stopping at Puckeridge, as Samuel Pepys recorded in his diary, but the other traffic must have helped to keep the village inns in business. The oldest of these is the 'Lamb and Flag' or 'Holy Lamb,' as it was called until about 1840 when the building previous to the present one was built. The Holy Lamb was the symbol of the Crusaders and the Knights of St. John are known to have been active around Standon.

Across the road from the 'Lamb and Flag' is an old timber framed house now called Cobwebs, that was formerly the 'Wagon and Horses.' Farther north, there was the 'Red, White and Blue,' now 'Barnacres' and across the road, 'The Plough,' that has been replaced by two new houses. The 'Fox and Hounds,' at the old Roman crossroads, is now a private dwelling but the pub name has been retained.

Plashes Wood is between Colliers End and Latchford and designated SSSI for the richness and diversity of its ancient woodland and is among the most important as well as largest woods in this part of the county (72 ha). The rich ground flora reflects the local variation in soil types (mixed acidic/calcareous).

It contains chiefly oak/hornbeam coppice with standards, with ash and beech, over bluebells and dog's mercury. It also has oak, ash, beech and silver birch over hazel, elder and blackthorn, as well as some coniferous plantation, marshy clearings and ponds. Though private, it is crossed by two public bridleways and skirted (on its eastern edge) by a public footpath.

About the Author

Ms. Sandor began her career working for John Denver's Music publishing company in New York as the Manager of Copyrights, Licensing, and Administration.

She appeared on the Sid Bernstein Show, Dolf De Roos and Cornerstone Cancer Center television commercials, and on the Jim Thompson WGCH, Deanna Spingola, and Conneaut Live! Radio Shows.

For seven years, she produced and hosted 'The Lady Rider Television Show,' 'Business Forum,' and 'Adventures with Cindy,' on Pinellas County Public Access TV.

Her writings have appeared in 'Guitar for the Practicing Musician,' 'The Greenwich Times,' and 'Tampa Bay News Times.' Her piece 'Europe to New York City on the United States – July 6, 1957,' published in the 50th *Anniversary Maiden Voyage Edition – S.S. United States Fastest Ship in the World* by Frank Braynard and Robert Hudson Westover, published by Turner Publishing Company.

She is a Travel Channel Academy Student and her independently produced videos have appeared on Anthony Bourdain's "What's Your trip?"

Ms. Sandor holds a B.B.A., with a minor in Human Development.

She is a past member of Palm Harbor Toastmasters #8248, and Phi Theta Kappa.

In December 2012, Sandor launched her first book "Through Innocent Eyes – The Chosen Girls of the Hitler Youth," a biography based upon her mother's secret journal from the time she was growing up in Austria during WWII. She lives in Tampa, Florida with her Chihuahua.

She is currently scripting a documentary to be filmed in Austria and Poland.

Additional copies of either book may be purchased by contacting the author directly at: http://www.cynthiaasandor.com.

CPSIA information can be obtained
at www.ICGtesting.com
Printed in the USA
LVHW040133091020
668359LV00014B/784

9 780999 755020